Cambridge Elements ≡

Elements in Politics and Society in Latin America
edited by
Maria Victoria Murillo
Columbia University
Tulia G. Falleti
University of Pennsylvania
Juan Pablo Luna
The Pontifical Catholic University of Chile
Andrew Schrank
Brown University

THE POLITICAL ECONOMY OF SEGMENTED EXPANSION

Latin American Social Policy in the 2000s

Camila Arza
CONICET and Centro Interdisciplinario para el Estudio de Políticas Públicas (CIEPP)

Rossana Castiglioni
Universidad Diego Portales

Juliana Martínez Franzoni
Universidad de Costa Rica

Sara Niedzwiecki
University of California – Santa Cruz

Jennifer Pribble
University of Richmond

Diego Sánchez-Ancochea
University of Oxford

CAMBRIDGE
UNIVERSITY PRESS

CAMBRIDGE
UNIVERSITY PRESS

Shaftesbury Road, Cambridge CB2 8EA, United Kingdom

One Liberty Plaza, 20th Floor, New York, NY 10006, USA

477 Williamstown Road, Port Melbourne, VIC 3207, Australia

314–321, 3rd Floor, Plot 3, Splendor Forum, Jasola District Centre, New Delhi – 110025, India

103 Penang Road, #05–06/07, Visioncrest Commercial, Singapore 238467

Cambridge University Press is part of Cambridge University Press & Assessment, a department of the University of Cambridge.

We share the University's mission to contribute to society through the pursuit of education, learning and research at the highest international levels of excellence.

www.cambridge.org
Information on this title: www.cambridge.org/9781009344111

DOI: 10.1017/9781009344135

First published 2022

A catalogue record for this publication is available from the British Library.

ISBN 978-1-009-34411-1 Paperback
ISSN 2515-5253 (online)
ISSN 2515-5245 (print)

Cambridge University Press & Assessment has no responsibility for the persistence or accuracy of URLs for external or third-party internet websites referred to in this publication and does not guarantee that any content on such websites is, or will remain, accurate or appropriate.

The Political Economy of Segmented Expansion

Latin American Social Policy in the 2000s

Elements in Politics and Society in Latin America

DOI: 10.1017/9781009344135
First published online: October 2022

Camila Arza
*CONICET and Centro Interdisciplinario para el Estudio
de Políticas Públicas (CIEPP)*

Rossana Castiglioni
Universidad Diego Portales

Juliana Martínez Franzoni
Universidad de Costa Rica

Sara Niedzwiecki
University of California – Santa Cruz

Jennifer Pribble
University of Richmond

Diego Sánchez-Ancochea
University of Oxford

Author for correspondence: Sara Niedzwiecki, saranied@ucsc.edu

Abstract: The early 2000s were a period of social policy expansion in Latin America. New programs were created in healthcare, pensions, and social assistance, and previously excluded groups were incorporated into existing policies. What was the character of this social policy expansion? Why did the region experience this transformation? Drawing on a large body of research, this Element shows that the social policy gains in the early 2000s remained segmented, exhibiting differences in access and benefit levels, gaps in service quality, and unevenness across policy sectors. It argues that this segmented expansion resulted from a combination of short- and long-term characteristics of democracy, favorable economic conditions, and policy legacies. The analysis reveals that scholars of Latin American social policy have generated important new concepts and theories that advance our understanding of perennial questions of welfare state development and change.

This Element also has a video abstract: www.cambridge.org/
Niedzweicki_abstract

Keywords: social policy expansion, universalism, outsiders, democracy, commodity boom

ISBNs: 9781009344111 (PB), 9781009344135 (OC)
ISSNs: 2515-5253 (online), 2515-5245 (print)

Contents

1 Introduction: Taking Stock of Social Policy Expansion in Latin America

In December of 2007, Evo Morales, Bolivia's first Indigenous president and leader of the leftist Movement for Socialism (MAS), approved the creation of a universal noncontributory pension named Renta Dignidad. Building on pre-existing programs, Renta Dignidad consolidated the right of every elderly person in Bolivia to a pension. "This is a social revolution ... We can become a model country in resolving social problems with our economic resources, and not with loans," Morales proudly declared during a visit to the small rural town of Warnes (Agencia de Noticias Fides, 2007). Elsewhere in Latin America, in countries as diverse as Argentina, El Salvador, and Peru, similar dynamics were at play in the early 2000s, as governments expanded access to income transfers and social services, incorporating sectors of the population that were previously excluded from such benefits.

After decades of retrenchment between the 1970s and 1990s, this expansionary phase spanned roughly the first twelve years of the twenty-first century and involved notable changes in the design of Latin America's social policies. Governments in the region created new programs in a variety of sectors, including health care, pensions, and social assistance, and expanded existing policies. Moreover, care emerged as a new area of state intervention for children, elderly people, and people with disabilities. Importantly, the recipients of these new policies were not only salaried workers, but also the previously excluded informal sector, low-income families, poor mothers, and domestic workers. Many of these policies contributed to a reduction of inequality across the region (López-Calva and Lustig, 2010; Gasparini et al., 2011). Some have referred to this period as the region's second wave of social incorporation (Reygadas and Filgueira, 2010; Filgueira, 2013; Rossi, 2015), while others have highlighted Latin America's leadership in defining new forms of social assistance (Barrientos, 2013).

These changes attracted significant academic attention, resulting in a growing literature on social policy expansion in Latin America. Research on the topic emerged in conversation with studies of social policy change in other regions and during other periods. The studies exhibit methodological pluralism, the collection of rich new data, sophisticated concept development, and innovative theoretical models. As a result, the literature generated important new knowledge, of relevance to experts on Latin America and beyond. The research provides insight into perennial questions of welfare state development and change, framing our understanding of the nature of social policy expansion and its political and socioeconomic determinants in new and innovative ways.

After two decades of scholarly production, it is time to take stock of the state of the field. This Element aims to do just that. Specifically, we analyze the existing literature on Latin America's social policy expansion during the early 2000s, seeking to identify key characteristics of the era and to explain how and why the expansion occurred. In doing this, we highlight the originality of this literature and identify new research agendas for the future.

What was the character of social policy expansion during the first decade of the twenty-first century? Why did the region experience this transformation and what lessons does the literature on Latin American social policy expansion offer for other parts of the world, including advanced industrialized democracies? This Element addresses these questions, providing an assessment of the state of the field and articulating what we identify as the central argument that emerges from the literature. Drawing on the existing literature, including our own contributions, we show that expansion during the early 2000s increased access to benefits for millions of previously excluded individuals, but that social policies remained segmented. We define segmentation as differences in access, benefit levels, and quality across class, gender, race, ethnicity, and immigration status. Expansion in the region was also uneven across policy sectors. We, therefore, describe the period as one of "segmented expansion."

The analysis also explores the literature about determinants of Latin America's social policy expansion. We argue that democracy provided the "motive" for expansion; the availability of resources – partly due to the "commodity boom" – provided the "opportunity"; and policy legacies shaped the segmented character of expansion. We find that Latin America's segmented expansion resulted from a combination of short- and long-term characteristics of democracy, favorable economic conditions, and policy legacies. Over the longer term, democracy generated a space for civil society organizations and some left parties to mobilize. With time, the growing strength of these pro-welfare organizations generated pressure for the expansion of social policies. In the more immediate term, increasingly intense electoral competition generated incentives for political elites to promise social policy expansion and abide by those commitments once in office. It also encouraged incumbent governments to expand existing social policies to a wider segment of the population, create new programs, or cover new social risks. These efforts were made possible by the availability of increased economic resources, thanks to a positive international economic environment. Social policy, however, remained segmented because of the ways in which existing policy shaped the distribution of power and public preferences, incentivizing reform in some sectors but not others. Policy legacies, therefore, reproduced existing inequalities in the design of new programs and in the extension of existing benefits.

This Element engages in a critical examination of the literature that analyzes Latin America's expansionary era, providing a reconstruction of how and why social policy was transformed. It is the result of an intensive process of collaborative work among six researchers across three different disciplines: political science, sociology, and political economy, who have researched different aspects of social policy expansion and change in Latin America. The authors come from academic institutions in Argentina, Chile, Costa Rica, the United States, and the United Kingdom. We surveyed findings from more than 250 academic articles, books, book chapters, and documents that study the expansionary period, published mostly between 2000 and 2021. The survey was focused on theoretical and empirical research.[1] Our aim was to critically review the scholarly literature that proposes concepts, typologies, and theories to explain trajectories of social policy expansion. The analysis of the literature was informed by our previous work. In other words, our diverse disciplinary backgrounds, expertise in sectors, and focus on different countries informed the conclusions about the literature's characterization of social policy expansion and its drivers. Drawing on the results of this analysis, we formulate an argument that seeks to synthesize the main findings in the literature. In this process, we purposely focus on the most salient scholarly arguments, highlighting points of agreement and, to a lesser degree, dissent. For this reason, we are well aware that we may have failed to include every argument in the literature, and that we may have unintentionally excluded important contributions.

The analysis of the literature presented in this Element is important for a variety of reasons. First, the expansionary era was, in many ways, successful with regard to social incorporation and poverty reduction. It was also a period in which Latin America led the way in many domains, such as the creation of conditional cash transfers (CCTs). Second, because this is an emerging literature, rooted in different disciplines, we still lack a comprehensive understanding of what we have learned about social policy expansion and its determinants in the region. Third, the theoretical and conceptual contributions of the literature on Latin America's expansionary era are important and could inform broader debates about welfare state development and change.

Scholars of Latin American social protection have innovated our understanding of policy expansion, highlighting the importance of not just program coverage, but also benefit generosity and service quality. It is through such a multidimensional lens that we identify the segmented character of Latin America's social policy expansion during the early 2000s. Literature on the

---

[1] We excluded descriptive studies that lacked a clear analytic focus, as well as studies that centered mainly on policy impact – including much of the extensive work published by international institutions.

region also made important advances in conceptualizing social policy universalism in ways that improve our analysis of social rights outside advanced industrialized economies. Previous to this scholarship, much of the literature ignored the specific situation of the Global South or grouped all countries together. Literature on the expansionary era also produced new and more precise ways of conceptualizing democracy and understanding its effect on the development and change of the welfare state. These theoretical advances will prove important for studies of social policy in both developing and developed countries.

Finally, given the waning of the commodity boom, the erosion of democracy, growing political discontent, and the COVID-19 pandemic, Latin America currently finds itself at a historical juncture that may involve rethinking the predominant economic model and redesigning social protection systems. For such a process to lead toward concrete improvements in residents' well-being, it is crucial that we develop a critical and comprehensive understanding of the accomplishments and shortcomings of Latin America's expansionary era.

In Sections 2 through 4, we discuss the concept of expansion and track its progress across the region. In Sections 5 and 6, we provide evidence from the literature that supports our explanatory framework and discuss other factors that deserve further study. We conclude with a discussion of the significance of our findings, highlighting the challenges that lie ahead as Latin America enters a period of economic crisis, democratic backsliding, and the effects of the COVID-19 pandemic.

2 Latin America: Historical Problems, Recent Expansion

Welfare states exist to address social risks, such as falling ill and requiring health care, growing old and exiting the labor market, losing a job, and earning too little to cover the basic costs of living. In market economies, social policy arrangements that address these risks represent a "second round" of resource allocation, following the distribution of land, financial assets, and, for most people, labor income. The main sources of financing social policy are general and earmarked taxes, on the one hand, and wage contributions from workers and employers, on the other. Each source of financing has specific distributional effects and is influenced in particular ways by labor market and macroeconomic policies. Decisions regarding how to finance benefits influence the policies' distributional effect and the ability to sustain or expand programs. They also shape potential alliances and conflicts among actors.

Altogether, such redistribution can accentuate, alter, or maintain inequalities that emerge in the "first round" of resource allocation. In Latin America, welfare regimes have been characterized by segmentation and dualism – a clear distinction between a relatively small group of formal workers and the rest of the population. Since the beginning of the twentieth century in the most developed countries of the region, and since around the 1950s in others, social policy followed a contribution-based model – usually referred to as Bismarckian. In this model, health services and pensions were provided through work-based social security. Formal workers were covered against an increasing number of social risks, while informal and self-employed workers, who make up a large portion of the economically active population across the region, were either excluded or had access to very limited benefits and lower-quality services. Inequalities among formal workers were also common, with some sectors, including military officers and public servants, exhibiting better protection than workers in other occupations (Mesa-Lago, 1979). This myriad of arrangements meant that social security in most countries had a limited – and sometimes even regressive – redistributive effect (Mesa-Lago, 1979; Barrientos, 2004; Filgueira, 2007). These shortcomings of social policy, coupled with a highly unequal distribution of labor income and assets, helped to make Latin America one of the most unequal regions in the world (Sánchez-Ancochea, 2021).

In the early 1980s, a debt crisis plunged the region into hyperinflation and recession, followed by fiscal austerity. During the subsequent two decades, the policy prescriptions of the "Washington Consensus" (Williamson, 2000) had a significant impact on social policy. Reforms during this period aimed at transferring part of the management of social risks to the market and reducing state intervention. Rooted in a concern about fiscal equilibrium and a criticism of the inequalities of the previous model, social policy reforms of the 1980s and 1990s involved the flexibilization of labor relations, the privatization of pension systems, an increased participation of the market in health care, a growing emphasis on targeting techniques to allocate social assistance benefits, and the decentralization of education and health-care services (Filgueira, 1998, 2013; Mesa-Lago, 2006; Huber and Stephens, 2012). Indebtedness and cuts to social spending in the 1980s and 1990s contributed to increasing poverty and inequality (Ruttenberg, 2019).

Things changed significantly during the first twelve years of the twenty-first century, a period of social policy innovation and expansion in Latin America. Notwithstanding regional heterogeneity, studies of social protection during this period concur that social policy gained ground in government agendas. In a context of economic prosperity, Latin American countries witnessed a remarkable expansion of transfers and services to incorporate informal workers and low-income families. This expansion included the easing of access to contributory programs (e.g. pensions), the extension of existing benefits (e.g. health care), the creation of new programs (e.g. CCTs and care services), broadening coverage (e.g. noncontributory pensions), and increasing social spending across policy sectors. As illustrated in Figure 1, between 2000 and 2018, public social expenditure as a percentage of GDP increased steadily from 8.5 to 11.3 percent and per capita social spending rose from 464 to 938 constant US dollars. Some latecomers performed even better: for example, per capita social spending by the central government increased fourfold in Ecuador, 150 percent in Nicaragua, and 98 percent in Paraguay, during the same period. This expansion entailed a wide-ranging development of social assistance programs, which shifted the balance between social insurance and social assistance, increasing the weight of the latter (Barrientos, 2011).

Access to benefits expanded significantly during the first two decades of the 2000s. As illustrated in Figure 2, the share of the population 65 and older who receive a pension benefit (contributory and noncontributory) increased from 51.5 percent in 2000 to 76.2 percent in 2017. Much of this increase reflected the creation of new noncontributory programs (Rofman et al., 2015; Arenas de

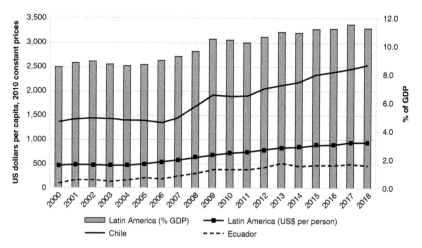

Figure 1 Latin America: Public social spending per capita and as percent of GDP, 2000–2018

Note: The figure represents central government spending. The Latin American average comes from the Economic Commission of Latin America and the Caribbean's (ECLAC) simple average of seventeen countries (Argentina, Bolivia, Brazil, Chile, Colombia, Costa Rica, Dominican Republic, Ecuador, El Salvador, Guatemala, Honduras, Mexico, Nicaragua, Panama, Paraguay, Peru, and Uruguay).
Source: ECLAC, CEPALstat.

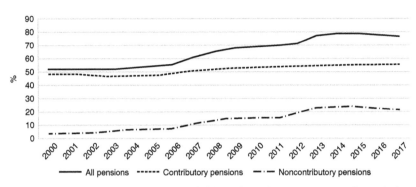

Figure 2 Latin America: Coverage of old-age benefits as a percent of population
aged 65+ (contributory and noncontributory)
Source: Arenas de Mesa (2019).

Mesa, 2019; Arza, 2019). A handful of countries, like Argentina, Bolivia, Brazil, and Uruguay, reached nearly full coverage, either with universal benefits (Bolivia) or through a combination of easing access to contributory programs while creating or expanding noncontributory ones (Argentina, Brazil, and Uruguay).

Progress in coverage, however, did not necessarily coincide with similar improvements in generosity, as new benefits were often small leaving a suffi- ciency gap between formal workers with contributory pension rights and individuals receiving noncontributory benefits. The benefit gaps that remained are evidence of the segmented character of social policy expansion during the 2000s – a fact that we focus on in Section 4.

Latin America has also pioneered the implementation of CCTs for families at the bottom of the income distribution. Almost all countries implemented these programs, which aimed to reduce child poverty by providing a small amount of income to families meeting certain conditions, such as school attendance and health checkups. Initially launched in Brazil and Mexico in the late 1990s, these programs expanded throughout the region quickly (De La O, 2015; Osorio Gonnet, 2018a, 2018b; Barba Solano, 2019). By 2011, eighteen countries in Latin America had such programs, covering a fifth of all families (Cecchini and Madariaga, 2011; Cecchini and Atuesta, 2017). As seen in Figure 3, individuals in recipient households covered by CCTs as a share of the total population increased from 3.6 percent in 2000 to 20.6 percent in 2016, with a peak of 22.6 percent in 2010. Most of these programs, however, were created separately from contributory family allowances or other social security benefits. This means that CCT recipients were incorporated in social assistance programs that were explicitly designed to serve poor families. This separation meant that poor and informal workers were not part of the same arrangements as

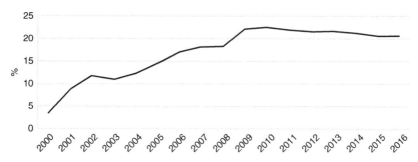

Figure 3 Latin America: People in recipient households covered by CCTs
as a percent of the total population
Source: ECLAC (2019b: 38).

formal sector workers, middle-income families, and the better-off (Antía, 2018; Arza, 2018a). As such, the policy innovation expanded access but maintained segmentation.

Expanded access to health care was particularly significant in countries that were neither the best nor the worst performers during the previous period: Colombia, Mexico, Peru, and, to a lesser extent, Ecuador saw notable improvements (Bonilla-Chacín and Aguilera, 2013; Montenegro and Acevedo, 2013). Changes in health care coverage were less significant in the countries that had already achieved relatively high access (Brazil, Costa Rica, Chile, and Uruguay) and in some laggards (Bolivia, El Salvador, Guatemala, Honduras, Nicaragua, and Paraguay). In countries that made the most progress, services were made available to millions of people, often for the first time, mostly through noncontributory programs. Expansion in those cases involved more generosity and equity, though important challenges persisted, particularly in terms of the most complex medical treatments. This left families at risk of having to pay for catastrophic care (Martínez Franzoni and Sánchez-Ancochea, 2018).

Expanded access to early childhood education and care (ECEC) programs was uneven across countries (Berlinski and Schady, 2015; Mateo and Rodriguez, 2015; Arza and Martínez Franzoni, 2018). A growing consensus emerged concerning the importance of these services for improving equality of opportunity among children, promoting economic efficiency, and facilitating the incorporation of women into the labor market (OECD, 2020). These ideas helped motivate efforts to expand services for children in low-income families (Blofield and Martínez Franzoni, 2014). Argentina, Chile, Colombia, Mexico, and Uruguay are cases of considerable expansion in this area (Esquivel and Kaufman, 2016). Between 2002 and 2012, coverage of early childhood education among children aged three to five increased from 39.5 to 79.5 percent in

Chile and from 63.5 to 82.6 percent in Mexico (OECD, 2020). However, even in countries leading this expansion, coverage of children under two years of age remained low and full-time services limited. Overall, these policies maintained segmentation in terms of the type and quality of services provided to young children. For those countries for which data are available, the share of children in full-time public services remained small during this period.[2]

A distinction between educational and care services also contributes to segmentation. As Staab and Gherard (2011) show, in Mexico, there are significant differences between preschools and day care institutions, which themselves vary significantly in quality, while in Chile, the inequality between the public and the private sector is particularly stark. Costa Rica and Uruguay stood out for launching nationwide care programs, which in the case of Uruguay, went beyond childcare to include elderly care as well. Overall, the framing of care as a public issue warranting a policy response, signaled a notable change in an area that, until recently, had largely been seen as a private, family affair.

By reaching people and risks previously ignored, the era of social policy expansion contributed to improvements in the distribution of income (Levy and Schady, 2013). According to Gasparini et al. (2016), the regional Gini coefficient (calculated as the unweighted average of fifteen countries) decreased from 0.54 in 2003 to 0.47 in 2012. The reduction took place across the board, with income inequality declining in every country except Costa Rica and Honduras (Sánchez-Ancochea, 2019). While roughly two-thirds of the reduction in inequality across the region resulted from changes in labor income due to the expansion of formal sector jobs, the increase in minimum wages, and the reduction in the skill premium (Lustig et al., 2016), social policy was also important. In Brazil, social policy contributed to almost half of the decline in the Gini (Barros et al., 2010; Alejo et al., 2014). If we considered the impact of improvements in the provision of services like health care, the impact of social policy on income distribution would probably be even higher (Lustig and Pereira, 2016).

3 Conceptualizing and Measuring Social Policy Expansion: Perspectives from the Literature

The process of social policy expansion in Latin America captured the attention of international institutions and researchers, who initiated new research programs, built novel datasets, and developed concepts and indicators to depict and

---

[2] Disaggregated data for part- and full-time services remain a challenge for state agencies that oversee public and private providers (Blofield and Martínez Franzoni, 2014; Berlinski and Schady, 2015; Mateo and Rodríguez, 2015). Even though most countries claim to have a national ECEC program with full-time hours, the proportion of children attending these services is not easy to calculate with existing data.

understand the changes taking place in the region. In this section, we focus on this burgeoning scholarship, identifying important dimensions analyzed in the literature to conceptualize Latin American social policy expansion. We also discuss the advantages and limitations of these efforts.

3.1 The Multiple Dimensions of Social Policy Expansion

Research on Latin American social policy has conceptualized and measured expansion in multiple but overlapping ways. In this section, we explore the strengths and weaknesses of different approaches and evaluate the extent to which they contribute to our understanding of social policy change. Table 1 summarizes the multiple dimensions of social policy expansion that are discussed in detail throughout this section.

The analysis of the existing literature helps us arrive at different dimensions of the character of social policy change in the region and constitutes the building blocks for our argument about segmented expansion. There are overlaps and contradictions in the literature between different categories; for example, some authors identify the coverage of new risks as part of access, while others would include it within generosity. In Table 1, we present the different dimensions of expansion in a stylized way, acknowledging that this is a first step in unifying the literature, but that more work is needed to arrive at an agreed-upon conceptualization of expansion and its different dimensions.

Table 1 Multiple dimensions of social policy expansion

Dimension	Definition			
Public social spending	Increasing fiscal effort for social protection (percentage of GDP and/ or percentage of total public expenditure)	Equity	The distribution of benefits across groups in the population (cuts across dimensions)	
Access	Coverage increase, incorporation of outsiders			
	New risks covered, new programs created			
	Nondiscretionary and more transparent allocation			
Generosity and quality	Higher cash benefit amounts			
	Higher grade of excellence of social services			

3.1.1 Public Social Spending

A first dimension that has traditionally been used to characterize and compare the reach and development of social policy, is public social spending. Public social spending indicates how much a country invests in the social protection of the population, and the evolution of social spending over time indicates progress or retrenchment in the public provision of benefits. The availability of public spending data across countries and over time has made this indicator one of the most widely used for comparative social policy analysis, especially in quantitative studies (Segura-Ubiergo, 2007; Haggard and Kaufman, 2008; Huber and Stephens, 2012; Zarate Tenorio, 2014; Niedzwiecki, 2015; Martín-Mayoral and Sastre, 2017; Flechtner and Sánchez-Ancochea, 2021).

There is growing consensus, however, that on its own, public spending does not provide a clear sense of social policy expansion, as it tells us little about whether resources effectively reach the target population, who benefits, and in what way. Public social spending could, for example, be used to subsidize private provision of social services, or to increase the value of pensions for privileged occupational groups, rather than expanding protection for low-income sectors.

Several decades ago, Esping-Andersen (1990) made a strong case about the need to go beyond the analysis of public spending, looking at other indicators that give a clearer sense of the distributional logic of welfare systems. He proposed the concepts of "decommodification" and "stratification" for comparing welfare regimes. Research on Latin American social policy has also moved beyond spending, adding a number of dimensions such as access and allocation mechanisms, benefit generosity, quality, and equity. Scholars have also built multidimensional measures that combine two or more of these dimensions.

3.1.2 Access

In recent scholarship on Latin America, access is the most widely used measure of social policy expansion. This is not surprising considering that large parts of the population have historically been excluded from both formal and effective access to benefits (ILO, 2021). Formal access refers to the existence of a legal right to a benefit. Maternity leave might be legally available for salaried workers yet not for the self-employed in some countries. Effective access refers to *actual* protection provided to individuals, taking into consideration labor market informality, bureaucratic weakness, and the uneven reach of the state across the territory, among other barriers.

The coverage rate – the most direct measure of effective access – has become the main indicator to assess and compare countries' social policy expansion. The exclusion of large segments of the population has been a defining characteristic of Latin American social security since its inception, as benefits were directed to insiders (formal salaried workers) but excluded outsiders (nonsalaried and informal workers) (Mesa-Lago,1979; Barrientos, 2004; Garay, 2016; Antía, 2018). Excluded sectors made up a relatively small group in a few countries, like those in the Southern Cone, where by 1970 social insurance had reached 68 percent of the population in Argentina, 76 percent in Chile, and 95 percent in Uruguay. However, in Central America, the excluded sector was very large. For example, by 1970, 96 percent of the population were excluded from social insurance in Honduras and 73 percent in Guatemala (Filgueira, 1998).

A key characteristic of the recent expansionary phase was the effort to reach out to "outsiders," and bring them into existing or new social programs (Carnes and Mares, 2016; Garay, 2016; Blofield, 2019; Cruz- Martínez, 2019). Drawing on this distinction between insiders and outsiders, which was first developed for social policy in the European literature (Rueda, 2005), Garay (2016) defines expansion as the creation of new social benefits or the extension of preexisting ones to a significant share (at least 35 percent) of the previously excluded population of outsiders. She argues that the expansion of nondiscretionary, large-scale, and stable social benefits to outsiders constitutes a breakthrough in the social incorporation of a group that previously lacked access to benefits. Barrientos (2009, 2013, 2019) has also written extensively about efforts to provide access to previously excluded groups and their implications for the character of the region's welfare model.

The literature on Latin American social policy has identified multiple barriers to access, and while some have been eliminated in recent decades, others persist. For instance, in the case of health care, even when the coverage rate is high, effective access may be less certain. Garcia-Subirats et al. (2014) illustrate this trend using municipal survey data in Brazil and Colombia, two countries with different health care systems but with a similar commitment to universal access. The authors find a multiplicity of problems that generate access barriers, from obstacles imposed by insurance companies and waiting times to insufficient human resources and health providers. While in Colombia barriers to effective access are related to the fragmented character of the health care system and the involvement of private insurance companies, in Brazil, they reflect the chronic underfunding of public services.

Besides incorporating outsiders into new or existing programs (horizontal expansion), access has also been expanded by increasing the types of risks covered (vertical expansion). One key example has been the creation of new programs or benefits, such as parental leave. Focusing on this double dimension of horizontal and vertical expansion, Castiglioni (2018) defines social policy expansion as the increase in coverage, the introduction of new or improved benefits, and/or the growing presence of the state in social policy provision and financing. In this case, the focus is not exclusively on the inclusion of the outsider population, but also on expansion in the scope of social policy (incorporating more people, more risks, or directing more resources).

Finally, removing access barriers also happens when benefits become nondiscretionary, that is, when they adhere to clearly defined and well-enforced legal standards. Discretionary benefits, by contrast, can be allocated based on clientelism or personal connection to a given official and therefore easily result in uneven access. Latin American countries have historically exhibited high levels of discretion in the allocation of benefits (Weitz-Shapiro, 2014), particularly in social assistance, so the movement away from such forms of administration, and toward legal guarantees and transparent criteria, constitutes a meaningful transformation in social policy.

Several authors have emphasized that the expansion of rights-based, nondiscretionary benefits in Latin America has strengthened the ability of citizens to know of, claim, and access benefits established in the legislation, marking progress in social incorporation (Cecchini and Martínez, 2012; Sepúlveda, 2014). Some recent scholarship sees this transformation as a form of expansion. Fairfield and Garay (2017) studied two "least likely" cases of redistribution, Mexico and Chile, under right-wing incumbents. Their evidence shows that both countries introduced new nondiscretionary, state-based social programs as opposed to inexpensive clientelistic benefits or private charity organizations indirectly linked to conservative parties. Pribble's (2013) conceptualization of universalism also considers the extent to which benefits are allocated in a transparent or discretionary manner, showing progress toward transparency in Uruguay and Chile in recent decades.

Although there have been clear advances in this area, not all social policies created during the expansionary wave were free from discretionary practices. De la O (2015) studies the expansion of CCTs between 1990 and 2011 and finds that while some governments established nondiscretionary policies, others implemented versions of CCTs that permitted political manipulation. Similarly, in their analysis of social programs aimed at aiding the poor, Díaz-Cayeros, Estévez, and Magaloni (2017) emphasize the diversity of policy outcomes in the recent period. Their work documents the expansion of social protection through four paths: clientelistic, entitled, universalistic, and failed. For the case of Mexico, they find that CCT beneficiaries are selected using objective criteria, with little room for individuals to self-select into the program or for politicians to prioritize their social base.

3.1.3 Generosity and Quality

Studies of Latin America's expansionary era focus on benefit generosity and quality, but there is disagreement about what the concepts mean. Much of the literature sees the two concepts as capturing similar dynamics, with generosity applying to transfers and quality to services, and we adopt this approach here. We note, however, that other authors differ, defining generosity as benefit levels, the number of benefits offered, or risks covered; and quality as the extent to which newly covered groups are adequately protected (e.g. Blofield and Martínez Franzoni, 2014; Martínez Franzoni and Sánchez-Ancochea, 2016).

The literature shows that generosity in transfers is a key dimension to assess social policy expansion in the 2000s. This is partly because many of the new benefits are determined administratively and are not linked to wage levels. This practice is different from the first wave of social incorporation (circa 1940–1970) that expanded social security benefits such as old-age pensions. These transfers were determined as a percent of past wages and, as a result, guaranteed a certain degree of sufficiency. By contrast, the noncontributory cash benefits that were expanded during the early 2000s were often not linked to wage levels nor to poverty lines.

Scholars have incorporated benefit generosity into the analysis of social policy expansion in various ways. Garay (2016) considers generosity to determine levels of inclusiveness. Comparing transfers provided to insiders and outsiders she concludes that in Chile and Mexico not only was coverage limited, but also most outsiders received a low benefit level, while in Argentina and Brazil, inclusive coverage was accompanied by a high benefit level. Pribble (2013) underscores that universalizing reforms reduced gaps in benefit generosity across the population; and Arza (2019) emphasizes that a focus on benefit generosity is essential to understand the nature and impacts of old-age pension coverage expansion during the early 2000s.

Service quality, in turn, refers to the level of excellence of the services provided, including the professionalization of staff in health-care and childcare services, the adequacy of infrastructure and equipment, staff-to-user ratios, and waiting times, to name a few indicators of "how good" services are. This qualitative dimension is a crucial, but understudied aspect of social policy provision, in no small part because comparative data are less available than for other dimensions such as coverage. By and large, studies addressing transfer generosity and service quality find that while some progress has been made on these dimensions, the region continues to exhibit significant gaps between contributory and noncontributory systems, as well as between public and private providers. These differences mean that, in general, countries in the region continue to provide disparate levels of social protection to poor and informal workers, as compared to middle-income and formal workers. All of this underscores the importance of looking beyond spending and coverage when assessing the character of Latin American social policy expansion.

3.1.4 Equity

Equity cuts across the three dimensions we have identified and refers to the distributive implications of social policy expansion: how spending, access, generosity, and quality are distributed across social groups (by gender, class, occupation, race, ethnicity, migration status, etc.). Equity can be a feature of policy outputs – that is, how social policy incorporates different groups in the population. Equity is also linked to policy outcomes – that is, what impact a particular policy has, for instance, on income distribution. Although the focus on equity is not new in social policy analysis, Latin Americanists have introduced innovations in its conceptualization and measurement during the past two decades.

One way in which several authors have addressed equity is looking at the distribution of coverage across the population. For example, using ECLAC's extensive data, Sojo (2017) disaggregates coverage of social insurance by income quintile, also considering the gendered distribution of access. She finds that the gap in access to health insurance between the highest and lowest income quintiles in 2013 was 36 percentage points compared to 43 in 2002. Meanwhile, in contributory pensions the 2013 gap was 49 percentage points, two more than in 2002. In both sectors, on average, coverage for women improved more than for men. Similarly, Arza (2018b) considers access to child-centered social policies in Argentina by type of program and income quintile. She finds that while new policies have increased access to cash transfers, health care and childcare, coverage remains stratified across income groups both in terms of the share of the population that is included and in the specific program (e.g. social insurance or social assistance, public or private) that each one has access to.

Equity has also been measured as difference in access and other conditions for the poor and nonpoor populations. For example, Ewig (2015) develops a holistic measure to compare changes in equity for three major health care reformers (Chile, Colombia, and Peru). Identifying four dimensions of equity (formal protection, stratification, real access, and performance), she concludes that in all three countries there was a convergence toward greater equity. Cotlear et al. (2014) also focus on health care, proposing a qualitative understanding of equity of services, considering the extent to which countries have overcome the institutional arrangements that separated the poor and the nonpoor.

Other authors also focus on equity in allocation in the analysis of social policy expansion. Altman and Castiglioni (2020: 769) define equitable social policy as "the extension of social services and benefits that further a fairer allocation to promote more equitable outcomes." Their operationalization of equitable social policy relies on an index that includes health equality, education equality, and reliance on means-tested versus universalistic programs.

Last, but not least, some scholars have linked the discussion of equity with the extent to which Latin American countries moved away from the market-oriented policies that dominated the region during the 1980s and 1990s. This discussion is partly related to benefit generosity and service quality. The extensive use of the market for social protection often affects equity negatively because only those who can afford private services get access to full and high-quality benefits. Market growth can also be a sign of preexisting inequalities, such as by providing only modest, insufficient services or protections that encourage most families who can afford it to shift to private provision. If coverage is incomplete, or generosity and quality are poor, it is likely that more families will purchase private services or insurance. By contrast, if states, for example, provide free childcare of good quality and opening hours compatible to what families require, it is less likely that families will need to use private childcare services.

Martínez Franzoni and Sánchez-Ancochea (2016) look at this issue in their analysis of universalism in the South by focusing on two crucial dimensions: provision (whether delivery is in public or private hands) and outside option (whether nonpublic options are available and how these are regulated). The role of public and private provision in social insurance and social services affects the character of expansion, as private systems tend to enhance individual provision and to link rights and benefits to one's ability to pay.

How the role of the market changed during the expansionary era is an open question that deserves further study. On the one hand, it is clear that the state expanded its role by increasing expenditures and access. On the other hand, reforms have not always aimed to undo the marketization of the previous decades, nor have the initiatives always introduced new and stronger regulations on private actors. The impact, therefore, has varied significantly by sector and cross-nationally. In some countries, pension reforms did reduce the role of the market (e.g. Argentina and Bolivia), but in most cases individual pension accounts continued to operate (e.g. Chile). In other areas such as health insurance, childcare, and long-term care, the role of the market continued to be significant, including during the expansionary era. In general, state regulation of private social services remained weak, even across countries with vastly different policy arrangements. Unlike the literature on the regulation of labor markets, research on social policy has focused almost exclusively on public provision, neglecting the issue of cross-national variation in state regulation of private benefits.[3]

3.2 Social Policy Expansion and Universalism

A large part of the comparative social policy literature assumes a dichotomy between targeting and universalism (e.g. Esping-Andersen, 1990; Korpi and Palme, 1998). Targeted programs aim at specific groups of the population. Most of the time, these are poor families in "need," who are selected using specific eligibility criteria and means-testing techniques, established in the social program's operational rules (CCTs are an exemplary case). Under this dichotomous understanding, universalism is the opposite of targeting, and universal programs are those that cover the entire population, independent of income and work status (universal health care systems are an exemplary case).

One of the important contributions from scholars of Latin American social policy has been to broaden our understanding of universalism, focusing on outputs rather than on policy design and rejecting the dichotomy of universalism versus targeting (Martínez Franzoni and Sánchez-Ancochea, 2016). In this approach, targeting is seen as a policy instrument that can promote or inhibit universalism. Martínez Franzoni and Sánchez-Ancochea (2016: 4) define universalism as a policy output that entails "similar, generous entitlements for all." Moreover, it must be established aside from the specific policy tools set in place to achieve those outputs. To establish degrees of universalism, they use a combination of three of the dimensions discussed previously: coverage, generosity, and equity.

Several other scholars have worked to conceptualize and measure social policy universalism in Latin America and apply it to the study of expansion during the 2000s. One early contribution to this agenda was Filgueira et al. (2006), who introduced the concept of "basic universalism." They define basic universalism as a set of policies that guarantee a minimum income and provide free or subsidized basic education and health services to all. Huber and Stephens

---

[3] An interesting exception is the work of Martínez and Maldonado (2019), which outlines a set of normative criteria to interconnect public and private arrangements.

(2012) draw on this definition to analyze redistributive social policy. The authors note that basic universalism is the most redistributive form of social policy in Latin America and define social policy expansion in terms of the adoption of basic universalism. A related discussion was also promoted by the Basic Income/Citizen's income literature, which analyzed the transformative power of guaranteeing all citizens a minimum income (e.g. Lo Vuolo, 1995, 2013) – a debate that acquired renewed salience in the context of the COVID-19 pandemic.

Pribble (2013) also offers a comprehensive analysis of social policy expansion in terms of universalism. She defines universalism as a social policy regime that provides all citizens with access to generous transfers and high-quality public services, delivered in a nondiscretionary way as a right of citizenship. In her view, recent reforms can be located along a spectrum that ranges from regressive to pure universalism. Her analysis finds that the expansionary era was characterized by progress toward universalism in some countries, though no Latin American state achieved pure universalism and outcomes varied across countries and policy sectors.

In a study of gender and social policy in Peru, Nagels (2018) also addresses universalism by focusing on coverage, quality, and equity of services. Like other authors, she treats universalism as a continuum. She concludes that despite reforms, the protection of social rights remained weak in Peru, with particularly adverse effects for women.

The concept of universalism, in its various forms and specific definitions, is linked to the concept of segmentation, discussed in Section 4. Martínez Franzoni and Sánchez-Ancochea (2016) regard segmentation as the opposite of universalism. Whereas universalism entails broad coverage and generous benefits that are equally distributed, segmentation comprises limited and unequal coverage and generosity. Pribble (2013), too, expects universalistic welfare states to be more effective at narrowing inequality and reducing segmentation.

3.3 Discussion

Scholars of Latin American social policy have produced pathbreaking work during the past two decades. With the goal of characterizing change in an unequal and diverse context, they have developed new analytic tools and innovative ways of measuring policy expansion. Some of this work relates to discussions in advanced industrialized democracies about insiders versus outsiders, but much of it has pushed the field in new directions, producing important innovations.

The new literature has responded to the complexity of social policy in the region. Countries have expanded social programs in different ways: some have focused on adding new groups to preexisting programs, while others have preferred to create new noncontributory programs for low-income groups. Some programs have put the emphasis in the generosity of benefits, while others have primarily focused on coverage.

All of this new work confirms a well-known but often forgotten insight: widely used indicators like spending and coverage, on their own, are insufficient to fully understand policy change and to provide meaningful comparisons across countries and over time. The expansionary effect of spending differs if it goes toward improving urban hospitals for the middle class or if it supports primary care clinics. Moreover, coverage expansion can reduce inequalities in social provision, or it can perpetuate them. In the context of Latin America's middle-income countries, there are new challenges in social provision. Whereas many countries have achieved universal access to primary education, for example, the quality of those services remains a significant challenge. For this reason, the increased focus on new dimensions and the use of multidimensional measures is a welcome innovation in the literature.

We find two contributions of this literature particularly promising for future studies of social policy in Latin America and beyond: the multidimensional approach to understanding expansion and the renewed focus on universalism. Moving beyond coverage and spending, a number of authors have highlighted new dimensions of policy expansion, particularly generosity/quality and equity, and developed innovative multidimensional measures for a more complete assessment of policy reform. In doing so, they have opened a new research agenda and an opportunity to evaluate social policy transformation and change. The multidimensional approach has also allowed scholars to identify instances in which a country advances on some dimensions, but not on others. On the other hand, scholars of Latin American political economy have advanced a more nuanced understanding of universalism, arguing that it is better understood as a continuum rather than as a dichotomous variable, which is particularly useful in the Global South, where few countries have pursued full-fledged universalism, but still vary significantly with regard to progress toward that end. All of this improves our understanding of social policy expansion and change. This is not only useful for analyzing the expansionary era, but also for the period of stagnation that has followed, including governments' social policy responses to the COVID-19 pandemic. We return to this point in Sections 7 and 8.

Overall, we find that scholars have developed new ways of conceptualizing and measuring social policy expansion. This diversity generates divergent conclusions about what actually happened during the expansionary era. In the next section, we present our own characterization of this period. We find that expansion during the early 2000s was segmented along the lines of social class, labor market status, gender, race, ethnicity, citizenship and place of residence, and uneven across policy sectors.

4 The Character of Policy Change: Segmented Expansion

The early 2000s were a period of social policy expansion in Latin America, particularly in terms of access. There was, of course, heterogeneity in the scope of this change, but the general trend toward increased access was clear. A key question, however, is the extent to which this expansion transformed the underlying character of Latin American welfare regimes, and if so, in what ways.

Drawing on studies of Latin American social policy change during the 2000s, including our own research on various countries, we argue that social policy expansion was significant but segmented across populations and uneven across policy sectors. Countries expanded access, public social spending, and in some cases, even the generosity of benefits, but policies have for the most part maintained different "lanes" of incorporation for different groups. Access has improved, but in a patchy and heterogeneous way and without a deep, structural transformation of existing welfare architectures. A fragmented social policy structure offers distinct benefits for insiders and outsiders, formal and informal workers, and the middle class and the poor. The segmented nature of social incorporation goes beyond labor market status to include other powerful stratifying factors such as gender, race, ethnicity, and immigration status.

To conceptualize segmentation, we draw on recent studies that have advanced the term. As Martínez Franzoni and Sánchez-Ancochea (2018) explain, the literature has used the term in two related but different ways: to depict compartmentalized social programs with more than one point of entry within the same policy realm (e.g. the separation of social insurance and social assistance in the provision of health care or family benefits), or as an outcome of social policy interventions. The two definitions are related – the existence of different programs will likely lead to unequal results – but refer to different levels of analysis: policy structures and policy outputs.

Martínez Franzoni and Sánchez-Ancochea (2016, 2018) focus on outputs, defining segmentation as the opposite of universalism. Segmentation occurs when there is limited coverage, low generosity, and low equity ; in other words, when a significant number of people are insufficiently protected, or when protection is unequal among different groups. Countries can of course make more progress in terms of one dimension, for example coverage, than others.

Other authors use the term segmentation to refer to the fragmented nature of social policy, focusing on unequal access to benefits. Segmentation occurs, for example, when salaried workers are entitled to health care services of higher quality than self-employed, rural, or domestic workers. Barrientos (2011) argues that "the spread of social assistance might have reduced the truncated nature of social protection, but this has been achieved by exacerbating segmentation. In most countries, social assistance is being institutionalized separately from social insurance" (Barrientos, 2011: 14). Similarly, as Cotlear et al. (2014) explain, the distinct funding and provision of health care services for the formal sector, the nonpoor informal sector, and the poor or vulnerable population, is a long-standing feature in most Latin American countries that produces segmentation.

Many authors have referred to segmentation, in one or both of these related ways, as a core characteristic of recent social policy expansion, which constrained a more profound and progressive change (Hunter and Borges Sugiyama, 2009; Barrientos, 2011; Ewig and Kay, 2011; Antía, Castillo, Fuentes, and Midaglia, 2013, 2015; Danani and Hintze, 2014; Antía, 2018; Arza, 2018b; Martínez Franzoni and Sánchez-Ancochea, 2018; among others). Other authors also highlight the limits of recent policy innovations in achieving transformative change (Lavinas, 2015, 2017; Lo Vuolo, 2016). Considering the different dimensions of social policy expansion discussed in Section 3, we argue that the progress is not equally distributed across the population, but is instead strikingly segmented by social class and labor market status, gender, race, ethnicity, citizenship, and rural versus urban status. Most countries have expanded access and public social spending, and to a lesser degree generosity. In most cases, however, states have maintained different "lanes" of incorporation for different groups of the population, thereby reproducing segmentation.

Segmentation along **social class and labor market status** is a key feature of Latin American social protection systems. It was one of the challenges that recent expansion aimed to address. The inclusion of informal workers in social protection systems, particularly as a result of the expansion of CCTs, social assistance pensions, and basic health services in some countries, narrowed previously existing coverage gaps across class and occupational status (Huber and Stephens, 2012; Cotlear et al., 2014; Antía, Castillo and Midaglia, 2015; Blofield and Martínez Franzoni, 2014; Anria and Niedzwiecki, 2016; Garay, 2016; Antía, 2018; Bernales-Baksai, 2018). According to Ocampo and Gómez-Arteaga (2016), health care and pension coverage among nonwage earners has experienced a marked increase. In fact, improvements in health have been more notable among nonwage earners, reducing or eliminating previous coverage gaps. However, even in countries that saw the largest increases in coverage, when we incorporate other dimensions (generosity and quality), progress in closing gaps and promoting equality across occupation and class categories is more limited. For instance, in the case of health care, the data show persistent and significant inequalities in the access to social protection by type of employment and income. Contributory coverage remained low and a significant portion of the population remained unprotected (Ocampo and Gómez-Arteaga, 2016). A similar pattern can be seen in old-age pensions, where coverage gaps were narrowed, but gaps in generosity between contributory and noncontributory benefits remained large (Arza, 2019).

Segmentation by **gender** has also been pervasive in Latin America. The impact of recent social policy expansion in reducing gendered inequalities in access to social protection has varied across sectors and countries. One of the main concerns in the literature that focuses on gender and social policy change is whether social policy promotes women's autonomy, weakening women's dependency on markets and on men, and altering the sexual division of labor. Determining whether such progress has been made requires that we measure the coverage and generosity of the benefits received by women, compared to those of men. It is also important to consider eligibility and the question of how women access benefits: as individuals, family members, or based on need. Arza and Martínez Franzoni (2018) assess the effects of the expansionary period on gender relations, focusing on old-age pensions, cash transfers, and care services. They find mixed results. Women improved their autonomous access to resources, weakening dependence on the market and male breadwinners. Gender gaps, however, are still wide, and are unlikely to close in the near future. These gaps can be seen in women's lower rates of pension coverage and smaller benefits; in the maternalistic design of CCTs; and in the underdevelopment of care services.

Molyneux and Gideon (2012) also show that the results of the expansionary period have been mixed when viewed through a gendered lens, though the authors note wide regional diversity. Staab (2012) shows that in Chile access to social programs expanded in three areas critical for gender equity: ECEC services, parental leave, and the introduction of child-rearing credits into the pension system. At least two of the three programs, ECEC and parental leave, did not depart from maternalistic traditions of Latin American social policy and fathers remain essentially absent. Similarly, Martínez Franzoni and Voorend (2012) analyze CCTs in Costa Rica, Chile, and El Salvador and find that, despite cross-national variation, these programs tend to reduce poverty and income inequality among women. The authors also note, however, that since the programs treat adult women as an instrument for reaching children, the policies have little impact on other aspects of gender-based power relations, such as respect, leisure time, marginalization, and exploitation of women's unpaid work. CCTs put money in women's hands, contributing to the decommodification of their material well-being, but in terms of eligibility, CCTs are maternalistic, and therefore, reproduce women's role as mainly or solely caregivers. The programs also have low levels of generosity and include time-consuming conditions that could conflict with women's labor force participation (Molyneux, 2006, 2009; Molyneux, Jones, and Samuels, 2016; Cookson, 2017).

These mixed results in terms of gender are also found across other policy sectors. For health care, Gideon (2012) shows that expansion in access contrasts with limited progress in mainstreaming gender into the health sector. For old-age pensions, Arza (2017) shows that pension reforms in Argentina, Bolivia, Brazil, and Chile, expanded access for women, with some countries also explicitly introducing gender equality measures. Still, gender gaps in access and generosity persist and many women only receive noncontributory benefits, which are considerably smaller than the benefits received by men. For care policy, the literature also suggests more progress in coverage than in reconfiguring gender roles (Blofield and Martínez Franzoni, 2014) and lower access to care services for poorer households (Faur, 2014). The reproduction of traditional gender roles also highlights the marginal role of fathers as subjects of childcare policy debates (Staab, 2012; Blofield, 2016) and policy measures (Blofield and Martínez Franzoni, 2014).

Segmentation by **race** and **ethnicity** has also persisted during Latin America's expansionary phase. In the early 2000s, Afro-descendent and Indigenous people had less access to health, education, and housing than White and Mestizo Latin Americans (Giuffrida, 2007; Mayer-Foulkes and Larrea, 2007; Romero and Orantes, 2017).[4] A handful of studies suggest that the expansionary period produced policy reforms that expanded access for Indigenous groups and Afro-descendants, but the authors note that deep racial and ethnic inequalities persisted.

Using an intersectional lens, Ewig (2018) shows that Bolivia's 2010 pension reform produced important gender-based gains, namely the equalization of life expectancy for men and women and a one-year contribution credit, per child for women. Still, the policy largely excluded the particular concerns of Indigenous women (Ewig, 2018: 454).[5] In the realm of education, Brazil, Colombia,

---

[4] For our purposes, mestizo populations are defined as people of Spanish and Indigenous mixed descent. The concept of *Mestizaje* has been used in attempts to unify the nation and had the effect of invisibilizing Indigenous and Black people in the region. Today, it manifests in the overall lack of historic data by race and ethnicity (Figueroa and Tanaka, 2016).

[5] Other authors have also emphasized the need to incorporate intercultural approaches to the study, design, and implementation of social policies (Correa Aste, 2011; Guendel, 2011).

Ecuador, Honduras, and Uruguay, adopted affirmative action policies, and this is considered a key prerequisite for promoting upward mobility among Afro-descendant and Indigenous people (Hernández, 2013). Brazil, in particular, has been a pioneer in adopting affirmative action programs, both at the municipal and federal levels, to reduce racial gaps in access to higher education and high-paying jobs (Telles and Paixão, 2013). While important, research shows that race-based differences in educational access continue to persist in Brazil (Vieira and Arends-Kuenning, 2019).

Health is another sector where racial and ethnic disparities have been particularly salient. These disparities are the result of multiple factors, including institutional racism, differences in income, level of education, poverty, and place of residence, just to name a few (Giuffrida, 2010). Racial and ethnic segmentation in health outcomes is common in Latin America, particularly in the realm of morbidity and mortality. Brazil, again, has been a pioneer in producing policies to fight institutional racism in the public health-care sector, including the Program to Combat Institutional Racism in Salvador de Bahia and *Quesito Cor* in São Paulo (Caldwell, 2017).

Indigenous populations, particularly those who live in isolated areas, face the challenges of lack of access to health services, adequate nutrition, and clean drinking water. These factors, coupled with higher rates of poverty, produce inequalities in health outcomes (Perreira and Telles, 2014: 248). Studying the 1980s–1990s, Ewig (2012) shows that access to social rights is particularly difficult for Indigenous women, due to the arbitrary approach to their sexual and reproductive rights in the context of the Peruvian health care reform. The alleged forced sterilization of some 300,000 mostly Indigenous women from rural areas was indeed the reason for pressing charges against former President Fujimori (1990–2000) in 2018 and for putting him on trial starting in March 2021. Disparities in health are also clear among Latin America's Afro-descendent populations. Ewig and Hernández (2009: 1149) analyze the effects of 1993 health reform in Colombia and find that by 2003, 53.9 percent of Afro-descendants had no health coverage compared with 32.9 percent of the population as a whole. Caldwell (2017: 11), in turn, finds that White Brazilians (*branco*) live, on average, six more years than Black (*preto*) and Brown (*pardo*) Brazilians.

Two studies by Nora Lustig and collaborators estimate the impact of public policy on Afro-descendant and Indigenous people in some Latin American countries. Considering the cases of Bolivia, Brazil, and Guatemala, Lustig (2017a) finds that these groups are overrepresented among the poor in all three countries. In Bolivia, the poverty rate among Indigenous people is 31.5 percent, compared to 14.7 percent for non-Indigenous groups. In Guatemala, the difference is even larger: 46.6 percent versus 20.6 percent. In Brazil, 14.6 percent of all Afro-descendants are below the poverty line compared to just 5.2 percent of the White population. Lustig shows that the combination of social transfers and direct taxes benefit Afro-descendants and Indigenous people, but the impact is small. Moreover, when considering the role of indirect taxes and other subsidies, the positive effect almost disappears in all three countries. In a study of Guatemala, Cabrera, Lustig and Morán (2015) show that noncontributory pensions and CCTs are beneficial to Indigenous people, while education and health have a smaller redistributive impact. Overall, the authors find that the impact of social policy on redistributing income in favor of Indigenous people remains limited. The average income per capita after taxes and social spending is 2.03 times higher for non-Indigenous people than for Indigenous people compared to a 2.13 ratio in the case of market income.

Overall, the literature suggests that expanded access to social policy during the early 2000s benefited Afro-descendants and Indigenous people, but coverage and benefit levels continue to be lower for those groups than for White and Mestizo Latin Americans. It is difficult, however, to draw firm conclusions, as the comparative literature has not generated sufficient evidence. More work is needed to evaluate concretely whether racial and ethnic segmentation decreased, remained the same, or even increased during Latin America's expansionary period.

Segmentation and the reproduction of structural inequalities are also evident in the persistent exclusion of international **immigrants** from social protection programs. The incorporation of immigrants is a challenge that has been largely overlooked in the literature on Latin American social policy, in part due to the limited availability of data. The massive movement of people across national borders challenges the "ideal type" of policy beneficiary mostly implicit in the literature (i.e. a citizen). Immigrants' segmented access to services and transfers is shaped by exclusionary policy requirements (e.g. long years of residency that put immigrants at a disadvantage), unequal incorporation to the labor market, and vulnerability that comes with a lack of legal immigration status (Niedzwiecki, 2021).

As was the case with race and ethnicity, social policy expansion has likely incorporated immigrants while maintaining segmentation between citizens and noncitizens. In Argentina, since 2004, the possibility to retire with fewer years of contributions and to pay the difference monthly (i.e. the "moratorium") increased overall coverage of contributory pensions, including the coverage of noncitizens. The reform decreased, but did not eliminate, the gap in access to contributory pensions between citizens and noncitizens. Specifically, the policy improved all residents' access to pensions, but coverage of foreign-born men was 9 percentage points lower, and foreign-born women 22 points lower, than the total population (Sala, 2017: 131–132). Along similar lines, focusing on thirty noncontributory pensions across twenty-eight Latin American countries, Cruz-Martínez (2019) finds that targeting mechanisms discriminate against immigrants, with variation across countries. He finds that social pensions in Cuba and Jamaica have the most inclusive eligibility criteria for immigrants, while programs in Colombia, Brazil, Guatemala, Paraguay, Uruguay, Bermuda, Ecuador, Panama, and Peru are the most "immigrant-unfriendly."

Segmentation by immigration status is also prevalent in health care, yet comparative data are scarce (Cabieses et al., 2013). For example, Noy and Voorend (2016) and Voorend (2019) show that a 2009 reform in Costa Rica made it more challenging for irregular and undocumented immigrants (especially Nicaraguan migrants) to access health care. Before 2009, immigrants could generally access free emergency care and could pay nonemergencies through their job or through a voluntary fee. After 2009, immigrants had to show affiliation with the Costa Rican Social Security Fund (CCSS) in order to be regularized, but afiliation with the CCSS required regularization. This created an impossible situation that contributed to the segmentation of immigrants vis-à-vis citizens, and differences across immigration categories. In 2013, while 13 percent of Costa Ricans lacked access to health insurance, 35 percent of Nicaraguan immigrants were in that situation (Voorend, 2019).

Segmentation by **place of residency across the territory** is also a long-standing problem of Latin American social protection systems, and one that has received increasing attention in recent years. A growing body research examines social policy implementation at the subnational level, uncovering evidence of uneven program delivery across the territory. These contributions call into question generalizations about social policy expansion during the first decade of the twenty-first century and point to the importance of considering not solely the design of social policies, but also actual implementation and effective access in order to gauge the extent to which all residents have access to benefits (Fenwick, 2009, 2016; Alves, 2015; Pribble, 2015; Giraudy and Pribble, 2018; Niedzwiecki, 2016, 2018; Giraudy et al., 2019).

Focusing on the expansion of primary health care and CCTs, Niedzwiecki (2016, 2018) finds that implementation has been uneven across the national territory. She studies the coverage of CCTs and health policies as a share of the targeted population across time in Brazilian and Argentine states and municipalities. The author finds that Argentina's CCT, *Asignación Universal por Hijo*, reached all poor families the first year it was implemented in the provinces of Santa Cruz and La Pampa, while in San Luis it reached fewer than 10 percent. In Brazil, *Bolsa Família* covered almost half of the target population in the

Northeastern states of Piuaí, Ceará, Rio Grande do Norte, Paraíba, and Alagoas in 2004. Conversely, in the states of Rio de Janeiro, Amapá, and Mato Grosso do Sul the CCT reached less than 15 percent of the target population. This means that access to CCTs is conditioned upon place of residence. On a similar note, Pribble (2015) finds that the effectiveness of job placement programs varies widely across Chilean municipalities.

Territorial inequality is a necessary qualifier of analyses of welfare expansion. Giraudy and Pribble (2018) show that when one adjusts national vaccine coverage by levels of subnational inequality in coverage, some countries appear to have made less impressive expansionary progress than conventional wisdom suggests. Similarly, Otero-Bahamon (2016) offers a measure of subnational inequality that challenges the dominant notion that expansion has been uniform and transformative, noting a new form of segmentation across subnational units.

In addition to expansion being segmented across populations and territories, it was also **uneven across social policy sectors**. For example, Holland and Schneider (2017) argue that expansion of noncontributory benefits has been quite widespread and relatively easy to achieve throughout Latin America, but other areas, such as social insurance and improvements to public service quality, are harder due to the complexity of the political coalition required to advance reform. The same happens with new areas of intervention like care policy, which compete for resources with other well-established sectors such as education and social security, as well as with policies considered more urgent or politically popular, such as cash transfers. In the same vein, Castiglioni (2018) shows that even within the same country and time period, social policy sectors may exhibit contrasting levels of expansion and outcomes. Pribble (2013) finds the same for universalism, demonstrating that progress was uneven across policy sectors.

Taken together, we claim that segmentation by class and labor market status, gender, race, ethnicity, citizenship, and place of residency remains significant in Latin America, despite more than a decade of social policy expansion. This empirical fact raises important questions about the extent to which the expansionary social policy reforms of the early 2000s effectively changed the unequal character of Latin American welfare systems. We find that despite advances in terms of coverage and benefit levels, social policy expansion has been unable to break with historical patterns of exclusion, dualism, residualism, and inequality. It also failed to entitle previously excluded populations of outsiders with meaningful rights and benefits, by guaranteeing adequate benefits, improving service quality, and/or expanding the range of social policy interventions to cover life course risks in a more comprehensive way.

5 Explaining Segmented Expansion: Democracy, the Boom, and Policy Legacies

Synthesizing existing findings, we argue that the combination of democracy and favorable economic conditions facilitated social policy expansion, but policy legacies fostered its segmented character. Democracy facilitated expansion because (1) it created space, over the longer term, for people and parties to organize and demand social benefits and (2) in the more immediate term, the presence of electoral competition generated incentives for political elites to expand policies. Favorable economic conditions during the early 2000s – a variable often mentioned in the literature but seldom fully explored – meant that there were resources available to respond to social demands without triggering the kind of distributional struggles or fiscal constraints that limited change in the past. Therefore, democracy and economic bonanza facilitated social policy expansion. However, policy legacies – including not only institutional rules, but also the practices, interests, values, problems, and politics they fostered – contributed to the maintenance of highly unequal social protection systems, both in terms of generosity of benefits and quality of services, producing segmented expansion.[6]

5.1 Democracy

Democracy facilitated social policy expansion in Latin America through long- and short-term mechanisms. Specifically, over the longer term, democracy generated a space for some civil society organizations and left parties to mobilize. With time, the growing strength of these pro-welfare organizations generated pressure for the expansion of social programs. In the more immediate term, increasingly intense electoral competition generated incentives for political elites to promise social policy expansion around campaigns, and abide by those promises once in office. It also generated incentives for incumbent governments to expand existing social policies to a wider segment of the population, create new programs, and cover new social risks.[7]

---

[6] In the process of constructing an argument that synthesizes the literature on the drivers of social policy expansion, we have focused our attention on areas of agreement between scholars, rather than disagreements. With this caveat in mind, this section and the next also highlight the most salient theoretical disagreements in the literature, including differing perspectives on parties, protest, and the role of international actors and ideas.

[7] We recognize that democracy and political competition can push social policy in a more expansive and universal direction, but that it can also result in segmented policy outcomes. In fact, the literature on Latin American political economy has shown that the effect of democracy during the twentieth century often remained limited or was even detrimental to social policy expansion, due to the problems associated with weak and nonprogrammatic political parties, institutional instability, clientelistic delivery of goods, relatively weak labor unions, and elite capture

5.1.1 Democracy's Long-Term Effects: Parties and Civil Society Organizations

Since the transitions of the 1980s, Latin America has enjoyed a period of relatively sustained democracy. Even before the expansionary phase, statistical analyses showed that cumulative years of democracy (in general, at least twenty years) tended to increase social spending, highlighting the importance of long-term processes of change (Huber and Stephens, 2012; see also: Haggard and Kaufman, 2008; Niedzwiecki, 2015). Huber, Mustillo, and Stephens (2008) find that democracies have a long-term positive impact on social security, health, and education spending. According to McGuire (2010), by protecting and providing freedom of expression, and increasing citizens' expectations of social rights, democracy provides a setting that allows for the expansion of benefits to marginalized sectors of the population. In fact, countries with more consolidated and longer tenured democracies, such as Costa Rica, Chile, and Uruguay, are also the countries that still today provide the most generous social policies (Segura-Ubiergo, 2007). During the 2000s, democracy influenced expansion over the long term by empowering left parties and collective actors (Huber and Stephens, 2012).

5.1.1.1 Democracy and Progressive Parties

The link between democracy, political parties, and welfare state expansion is well established in research on Western Europe. According to the power resource perspective, the presence of strong social democratic parties that rely on the support of organized workers was crucial for the emergence and expansion of the welfare state. In this approach, democracy is taken for granted and considered a prerequisite: it is the only political regime that makes it possible for progressive political parties and workers to organize, access power, and push for new or better benefits (e.g. Korpi, 1989; Esping-Andersen, 1990).

Some authors studying expansionary social policy in Latin America during the "pink tide" (Smith, 2012) or left turns, in plural (Cameron, Hershberg, and Beasley-Murray, 2010), take insight from the power resource perspective, highlighting the ways in which sustained democracy in the late twentieth and early twenty-first centuries created a space for left parties to grow and expand

(e.g. O'Donnell, 1994; Calvo and Murillo, 2014; Weitz-Shapiro, 2014; Tillin and Duckett, 2017: 265; Brinks et al., 2019). We contend that segmented outcomes are not the direct result of democracy, per se, but rather the product of democratic competition that plays out in a context of segmented policy legacies. In other words, we find that political competition is most likely to produce segmentation when the design of existing policies, or policy legacies, empower certain actors, grant special privileges, and generate preferences that favor the maintenance of segmented policy design. For this reason, we focus our attention on the ways that policy legacies, rather than democracy, influence segmentation.

their reach. Huber and Stephens (2012: 32) apply the expectations regarding policy preferences of European left parties and argue that these "travel relatively well to Latin America," as left parties in Latin America also favor redistributive social policies that benefit underprivileged citizens.

The research by Huber and Stephens (2012) and a handful of other authors cover a longer time period than the expansionary phase. This work confirms that democracy and left party strength influenced social policy expansion, both historically and during the early years of the twenty-first century. Huber and Stephens (2012) show that sustained democratic rule in Latin America allowed for the development and electoral victory of the left, which, in turn, facilitated social policy expansion. Democracy and the presence of the left in government serve to balance the distribution of power and allow social demands to emerge, ultimately producing more egalitarian policies. Similarly, Huber and Niedzwiecki (2015, 2018) highlight the role of left parties in the social policy expansion witnessed in Argentina, Brazil, Chile, and Uruguay during the early 2000s.

Madrid, Hunter and Weyland (2010) argue that one of the central goals of left-wing parties in Latin America has been to promote social justice. In this way, "even within 'well-defined structural and institutional constraints,' left governments are ideologically committed to improving social inequalities and expanding social citizenship rights" (Cook and Bazler, 2013: 4). Along similar lines, Ciccia and Guzmán-Concha (2018) show that the strength of left-of-center parties in Congress was an important factor for the generosity of social policies directed toward outsiders. Borges Sugiyama (2013), in turn, notes the crucial role of this actor for the diffusion of programs across municipalities in Brazil. Overall, when left-wing parties were relatively strong, social policy expansion was possible (Huber and Pribble, 2011; Huber and Stephens, 2012; Anria and Niedzwiecki, 2016; del Pino, Sátyro, and Midaglia, 2021).

All this literature is, in our view, convincing and many of these works illuminate different causal processes and add nuance to the relationship between party ideology and social policy expansion. Pribble (2013), for example, contends that the character of political parties helps explain why some countries ruled by left parties progressed further toward universalism than others. She defines party character as the combination of three characteristics: the strength of ties between the base and elites; the nature of the external linkage mechanism, namely whether it is programmatic or nonprogrammatic; and party ideology. Combining these three characteristics, Pribble (2013) identifies four types of parties located on each side of the ideological spectrum. She finds that constituency-mobilizing and elite electoral parties of the center-left, such as the Frente Amplio in Uruguay and the center-left parties in Chile, are the most likely to pursue universalistic social policy. Pribble (2013) argues that the Frente Amplio's strong connection with its base meant that elites were pushed to pursue more universalistic policy. In Chile, center-left parties' programmatic connection with voters incentivized advancement toward universalism in health and pensions, but the absence of a strong push from below meant that the efforts were sometimes more limited in scope than in Uruguay. The study reveals that nonprogrammatic electoral parties, such as the Socialist Party of Venezuela, were less likely to pursue universalistic expansion, especially in health and education. In the case of Venezuela this was because the party's reliance on the charismatic appeal of Hugo Chávez encouraged the creation of parallel state institutions, which drained state resources and segmented benefits.

That democracy created a setting in which left parties could grow, ultimately winning elections and expanding social policy, does not negate the fact that democracy can also empower the right. Some of the existing literature finds that right-wing parties have also occasionally expanded social policy (Garay, 2016; Fairfield and Garay, 2017). For example, Fairfield and Garay (2017) show that Mexican Presidents Vicente Fox (2000–2006) and Felipe Calderón (2006–2012), and Chilean President Sebastián Piñera (2010–2014), introduced pro-poor social policies and increased taxation targeting elites, regardless of their ties to the business sector and their own preferences for less government. In an analysis of Latin American CCTs, De La O (2015) argues that both right and left presidents introduced expansionary policies. Taking insight from the cases of Argentina, Colombia, Guatemala, Peru, and Mexico, she shows that the decision to create nondiscretionary transfers depends on whether the president faces opposition in Congress, independent of ideology. In contexts of strong opposition, presidents will be forced to adopt CCTs that tie their own hands, while CCTs designed in a setting of weak opposition are more likely to exhibit discretionality. Likewise, relying on panel data from eighteen Latin American countries between 1990 and 2013, Altman and Castiglioni (2020) show that once alternative explanations are included, the ideological leaning of governments loses statistical significance to explain the expansion of equitable social policy.

We contend that the expansion of social policy under right-wing governments does not contradict the crucial role of the left. When electoral competition is tight, right-of-center parties will strategically adapt to the relative ideological placement of the leading antagonist party. When such a party is located to the left of the ideological spectrum and has a significant share of seats in the legislature, social policy expansion under right-wing parties has been more salient (Castiglioni, 2020). This view is consistent with the findings of scholars analyzing European social policy. According to Hicks (2009), for example, there is evidence from advanced industrial democracies that when right-wing governments confront an electorally consequential left, they move in a pro-welfare direction, something that has been named the "left contagion."

Additionally, when thinking about the role of ideology, we must consider not only the magnitude of expansion, but also the kinds of expansion that took place. Latin America's right-of-center governments adopted social policies that, more often than not, did not challenge critical elements of the market-oriented logic, such as means testing, targeting, reliance on private providers, and fiscal conservatism. According to Castiglioni (2020) a quick review of expansionary social policy under right-of-center governments allows us to identify at least three key trends. First, during the expansionary period, all countries led by right-wing governments introduced some sort of noncontributory transfers, even those that previously exhibited a clear insufficiency in the realm of social protection, such as El Salvador under Elías A. Saca (2004–2009), Panamá under Ricardo Martinelli (2009–2014), and Paraguay under Nicanor Duarte Frutos (2003–2008). In those cases, expansion tended to rely on CCTs and/or subsidies directed to specific, vulnerable groups. These policies are appealing for right-wing governments because they allow for targeting resources to the poor and "deserving" beneficiaries, such as children, and also because they are considered cost-effective and market compatible (De la O, 2015: 4). Left-wing governments have also created and expanded CCTs, but for different reasons. As De la O (2015) explains, the left endorses these programs because they promote redistribution and social inclusion, are easier to deliver than in-kind subsidies, and allow beneficiaries to decide how to use the transfers.

Second, some right-of-center governments expanded contributory transfers as well. The best example of this trend is captured by Chilean conservative President Sebastián Piñera (2010–2014), who expanded maternity leave. As a result of the reform, Chile enjoys the most extensive maternity leave in the region (more generous than several industrialized democracies). According to Castiglioni (2019), Chile's conservative parties expanded this policy in a context of competitive elections and challenges from the left. Piñera's reform was also motivated by conservative ideology. As Blofield and Martínez Franzoni (2014) show, the design of the program reinforces conservative beliefs that childcare is primarily a maternal responsibility. In other words, Piñera's expansion of maternity leave strengthened the right's approach to work – family conciliation. This differs from the approach of progressive parties, which seek to offer publicly funded services to transfer care work outside the family.

A third and final trend among right-of-center governments relates to the expansion of social services. The case of Colombia clearly illustrates this trend. Conservative President Álvaro Uribe (2002–2010) significantly expanded contributory and noncontributory health care coverage. The reform contained five key components: individual insurance, regulated competition among providers, the possibility for beneficiaries to select insurers, state subsidies for low-income individuals, and a state-defined package of services (Ewig, 2015). Despite the gains in coverage, Colombia followed a path of segmented expansion that failed to reduce the existing differences in benefits and service quality between those affiliated with the contributory and the subsidized regimes (Cotelar et al., 2015; Uribe-Gómez, 2017).

5.1.1.2 Democracy and Collective Actors

An established record of democracy helps collective actors, such as unions and social movements, flourish, thereby opening the possibility that such organizations might influence social policy expansion.[8] Latin Americanists have made several contributions to the literature on democracy, social movements, and social policy, much of which is particularly relevant in the context of social policy expansion. Pribble (2013) and Garay (2016) show that social policies that receive societal input tend to be broader in their inclusion of outsiders and more generous than policies that remain in the exclusive realm of elite decision-making. According to Garay (2016), social policies that receive input from social movements or respond strategically to their demands tend to expand coverage and benefits more than social policies that only respond to electoral pressures. In a similar vein, Ciccia and Guzmán-Concha (2018, 2021) analyze the effect of collective mobilization on the propensity of Latin American governments to introduce expansionary policies favoring outsiders – one of the most significant innovations during the 2000s. They conclude that countries that exhibit more protests have produced more universalistic reforms (Ciccia and Guzmán-Concha, 2018). Blofield et al. (2017) show that domestic gender equality activists pushed left governments to place gender equality in social policy on the agenda. Finally, Altman and Castiglioni (2020), Wampler, Borges Sugiyama, and Touchton (2019), and Gibson (2019) show that civil society strength and participation are important for the expansion of social policy.

Niedzwiecki and Anria (2019) focus on the different forms that civil society participation can take – either through "inside" or "outside" state channels. They show that in Brazil, popular participation in health care before the

---

[8] This does not mean that democracy always strengthens organized civil society, nor that social movements always pressure for social policy expansion.

commodity boom took place "inside" the state's formal channels, such as participation in the bureaucracy or in conferences and councils (Falleti, 2010). The authors stress that implementation of health care in Brazil was highly participatory throughout the expansionary period. In Bolivia, by contrast, attempts to influence pension reforms in the 2000s occurred predominantly via "outside" channels, by coordinating pressure in the streets (Anria and Niedzwiecki, 2016). At a more general level, Silva (2015: 35) argues that Bolivia and Ecuador mobilized Indigenous groups and facilitated the integration of Indigenous people "into a system of substantive rights focused on expansive social policy." The effect of ethnic movements on social policy expansion deserves further attention in the literature. While some literature has focused on the intersection of ethnicity and gender (Ewig, 2010), the ways that racial, ethnic, and gender identities shape the mobilization of demands for policy expansion and state responses to social grievances, has remained underdeveloped.[9]

Labor unions have also, at times, been key actors in social policy expansion. Garay (2016) argues that unions presented three possible positions toward expansion: support, indifference, or opposition. With regard to the support strategy, she shows that social movements were more successful in demanding expansion when they formed coalitions with unions. Such insider–outsider coalitions characterized expansionary reforms to outsiders in Brazil and Argentina prior to the commodity boom and left turn. Anria and Niedzwiecki (2016) show that a similar dynamic played out in Bolivia with the case of Renta Dignidad, the noncontributory pension reform that was approved by left-wing President Evo Morales in 2008. The authors find that unions and grassroots organizations coordinated pressure in the streets to secure approval of the pension reform.

In other cases, unions were indifferent to expansion, particularly when reforms did not immediately affect the benefits for their affiliates. A third possible position of unions toward expansion was one of opposition. Garay's (2016) example of opposition includes President De la Rúa's attempt to eliminate family allowances for formal workers earning higher salaries and reallocate those funds for family allowances to outsiders in Argentina. In cases like this, in which expansion includes an explicit cutback for "insiders," or threatens their rights, opposition is more likely. Unions representing civil servants in Brazil also opposed leftist President Luiz Inácio Lula da Silva's proposals to decrease benefit stratification between insiders and outsiders by imposing benefit

---

[9] Caldwell (2017) is an important exception by analyzing the role of Black Women's movements, Feminist Movements, and Black Movements in visibilizing the health, racial, and gender disparities in Brazil's health care system.

ceilings, which would have especially punished civil servants who have higher pensions. In July 2003, for example, more than 4,000 civil servants participated in a march in Brasília, calling the legislators who supported reform measures "traitors" (Niedzwiecki, 2014).

While unions may be supportive, indifferent, or in some cases even oppose social policy reforms that seek to expand access to outsiders when their rights are at risk, research based on quantitative data for a longer-term period generally finds that organized labor had an independent and positive effect on social spending. Zarate Tenorio (2014) analyzes Latin American countries from 1970 to 2007 and finds that strikes have a strong and positive effect on social security and welfare spending. Union mobilization does not, however, affect education or health spending. Niedzwiecki (2015) measures union strength differently, through union density, minimum wage, and the degree of organizational concentration. The author finds that spending on social security/welfare and health is higher in countries where unions are strong. Overall, quantitative studies reveal the positive effect of unions on social spending, but without systematically incorporating their effect on segmentation.

5.1.2 Democracy's Short-Term Effects: Electoral Competition

In addition to long-term effects, democracy has also influenced social policy expansion via shorter-term mechanisms, specifically through the intensification of electoral competition at all levels of government. Latin America's experience during this period reveals that competitive elections tend to promote the expansion of social policy.

Several studies emphasize the role of electoral competition in explaining the recent expansionary phase. In the health sector, Ewig (2015) finds that growing competition generated convergence toward greater equity in Brazil, Chile, and Colombia. In a similar vein, Pribble (2013) shows that in Argentina, Chile, and Uruguay, the more intense the electoral competition, the more likely governments were to propose and expand social policies. She further argues that it matters whether parties face electoral competition from the left or the right of the ideological spectrum. In the case of Uruguay, for example, the growing strength of the left-leaning Frente Amplio pushed the center-right traditional parties to pursue social policy expansion in the mid-late 1990s.

Electoral competition interacts with the growth of outsiders to explain the expansion of noncontributory programs. As Carnes and Mares (2014) show, market-led economic reform resulted in increased informality, social vulnerability, and labor market volatility. As a result, the number of people without protection from traditional contributory programs increased and the demand for noncontributory programs became increasingly hard to ignore. Political parties from the left and the right faced incentives to expand noncontributory programs to respond to these demands. Accordingly, competitive scenarios may push political parties to seek the votes of outsiders, thus engaging in reforms that expand social policy to those sectors (Garay, 2016; Fairfield and Garay, 2017; del Pino, Sátyro, and Midaglia, 2021). More broadly, electoral competition has been a key force behind the expansion of equitable social policy across the region (Altman and Castiglioni, 2020).

5.2 Favorable Fiscal Conditions

Without equitable and sustainable funding, it is hard to maintain the long-term expansion of social programs – a point that Pribble (2013) highlights in her work on universalism. Yet, as Fairfield (2015) shows, it is politically difficult to raise taxes and this has often limited governments that would otherwise have sought to expand social spending. In much of Latin America, the tax burden remains low compared to other regions and to countries with similar levels of GDP per capita. In this context, finding additional income sources that avoid conflict over taxation makes social policy expansion more feasible.

This is what happened during the expansionary era. From the beginning of the new millennium through roughly 2013, Latin American countries faced an exceptional international economic environment. Increasing demand for and the international prices of Latin America's commodity exports received ample attention in the political economy literature, with several authors emphasizing that the positive terms of trade freed up resources. This, in turn, allowed for the expansion of social programs (Levitsky and Roberts, 2011). This positive impact was particularly significant for the years 2003–2008, a period that ECLAC has called "Latin America's Six Golden Years" (*el sexenio de oro*), not only because of the patterns of growth and fiscal surplus, but also because forty-one million people rose out of poverty (Montaño, 2011: 15). The surplus generated by the economic bonanza decreased the need to rely on external financing and abide by its conditionalities, thus allowing left presidents to pursue their preferred domestic policies (Murillo, Oliveros, and Vaishnav, 2011: 53). Grugel and Riggirozzi (2018: 555) echo this argument, noting that "the reasons the Left was able to extend welfare and avoid borrowing was the long global commodity boom that lasted from December 2001 until June 2008." Higher export prices increased public revenues by expanding the amount of rents in the hands of the state, by contributing to higher economic growth, and by increasing tax revenues (CAF, 2013).

Yet focusing on the commodity boom as the only positive factor to help finance expansion is problematic, since not all Latin American countries benefited from it. When evaluating the evolution of the terms of trade during the period 2003–2013, it is possible to identify three different sets of the countries: (1) those in which the terms of trade improved significantly (Argentina, Brazil, Ecuador, Peru, Colombia and, especially, Bolivia, Chile, and Venezuela); (2) those in which the terms of trade did not change (Mexico, Paraguay, and Uruguay); and (3) the six Central American countries and the Dominican Republic where the terms of trade actually declined (Ocampo, 2017). Given that all these countries to some extent expanded social policies, yet not all of them benefitted from commodity booms, it is important to highlight the role of other sources of favorable economic conditions, such as low interest rates and a large supply of international loans (Campello, 2015; Dorlach, 2020). For example, under President Mauricio Funes (2009–2014), a foreign loan made it possible for El Salvador to expand its health care infrastructure as well as to create the Universal Social Protection System. In Guatemala, a far-reaching CCT program during the administration of Alvaro Colom (2008–2012) was financed by a combination of domestic revenue and foreign loans (Martínez Franzoni and Sánchez-Ancochea, 2015).

Of course, the process of transforming the new resources into social policy expansion was not automatic. Most of the literature agrees that increased revenue could have been used for a range of purposes and the degree to which it was directed to social policy depended to a large extent on politics. Although most of the existing literature on Latin America's expansionary phase assumes that favorable economic conditions facilitated social policy growth, it has failed to theorize the mechanisms that explain this outcome. In this Element, we contend that mobilized demands for redistribution, tightly fought elections, and increased access to revenue all combined to facilitate social policy expansion during the early 2000s.

A key question is whether electoral competition and growing demands for redistribution also triggered meaningful tax reforms or not. Authors like Bird and Zolt (2015: 323) believe that many countries secured a new tax contract that reflected increased democratization, expansion of the middle class, and the emergence of center-left governments. Progressive taxes did increase across the region, and the regressive character of tax systems decreased in many countries (Cornia et al., 2014; Sánchez-Ancochea, 2019).

Yet overall, there are more reasons to believe that the increase in revenue was primarily driven by external forces and not by meaningful reforms. Bergman (2019) shows that Latin American states made no significant efforts to improve income tax collection during the commodity boom because high export earnings and intense electoral competition dissuaded parties from investing in improved compliance. Some studies show that the commodity boom explained most of the growth in tax revenues in South America (CAF, 2013). Mahon (forthcoming) finds a 0.86 positive correlation between commodity prices and central government revenues for the period 1990–2016 but no correlation in OECD countries. Most of this positive relationship results from higher prices in the 2000s: In fact, the correlation coefficient for the 1990s is only 0.35. Doyle (2018: 18) shows that the strategy of using commodity export revenues that many left-wing governments were able to use during the 2000s became unfeasible with the Great Recession. We return to this point in Section 7.

Moving forward, we believe that the relationship between funding sources and the financial sustainability of social policy would benefit from further study. In order to do so, the growing literature on tax reform and the determinants of tax policy (e.g. Fairfield, 2015; Flores-Macías, 2019) would need to be better integrated with studies of social policy expansion and its determinants. There is little systematic analysis of the extent to which tax increases were driven by social policy needs and/or made the expansion of new programs more likely. Similarly, there is little exploration of whether gains in social policy made during the expansionary phase facilitated tax collection by improving public goods, and by extension, the persuasive power of the state to encourage citizens and firms to submit to taxation. In exploring these issues, future studies could draw inspiration from Fairfield and Garay's (2017) exploration of the links between taxes and social policy. The authors analyze the experiences of Chile and Mexico to show how social policy demands created pressures on the tax front and how higher commodity prices served to weaken the influence of the business elite on social policy reforms.

5.3 Policy Legacies and Segmented Expansion

Virtually all the research on Latin America's expansionary phase sees the design of previous policy, or policy legacies, as a crucial determinant of the character and scope of expansion. Indeed, there is strong agreement with Pierson's (2000) influential study, which emphasizes the fact that "history matters" when attempting to reform the welfare state. While Pierson's work does not analyze Latin America and was originally focused on how legacies constrain options for social security reform (Pierson, 1994), studies of social policy in Latin America have drawn heavily on his concept, finding evidence that policy legacies shape the success and content of reform efforts. We argue that policy legacies account for the segmented character of social policy expansion in the early 2000s that we described in Section 4.

Our focus on the impact of policy legacies in segmenting expansion is not to say that electoral competition, political parties, or the power of organized interests are inconsequential in generating inequities, but rather that the design of previous policies is critical for understanding why political processes play out in ways that reproduce inequality. We argue that policy legacies create the context in which the politics of social policy expansion unfolds. It is, therefore, essential to consider the design of existing policy in order to understand the segmented character of expansion during the 2000s. Specifically, policy legacies in the region generated segmentation by creating popular policies that were hard to change, by strengthening constituencies and stakeholders that protected their privileged position and opposed redistributive reforms, by institutionalizing gendered and territorial hierarchies, and by generating pressure to act in some sectors rather than others.

The popularity of previous policies encouraged segmented expansion. As we discussed in Section 2, social policy in most Latin American welfare states prior to the early 2000s was highly segmented, with some groups excluded and others incorporated with different degrees of generosity. This kind of system enjoyed strong support from individuals who had access to benefits. The existing programs built interests, expectations, and demands to sustain that protection. Given the popularity of preexisting programs, policy reforms in the early 2000s tended to increase access through the creation of new programs, thus maintaining segmentation in the generosity of benefits and quality of services. As Arza (2018a) documents, this is what happened with the expansion of child benefits to previously excluded groups in Argentina, Brazil, and Chile. Similarly, Staab (2016) shows that in Chile, President Michelle Bachelet (2006–2010) was only able to introduce incremental change to the social protection system, despite enjoying an unprecedented mandate. This was due to the limiting role of policy legacies and political institutions, which inhibited the extent to which this mandate could be translated into concrete outcomes. In this way, Latin America's expansionary phase provides evidence of how policy legacies can curtail deep, structural reforms that might break with preexisting inequalities.

Perhaps the most significant reason why policy legacies produced segmented expansion is because policies and stakeholders that emerged from previous configurations of social protection limited the scope of options available for future policy change. This happens because previous policies generate interest groups and empower some actors, while limiting the voice and power of others. In Latin America, this is a significant driver of segmentation, not only between formal and informal workers but also among formal workers. During the expansionary phase, beneficiaries of existing policies often resisted the unification of programs, which led to the creation of complex systems with separate benefits.

Policy legacies are also a key factor explaining the continued role of the private sector during the expansionary phase. An example of this can be seen in health reforms in Chile, Uruguay, and Argentina. In Chile and Uruguay, while the new systems expanded access to public services, the initiatives maintained the existing public–private dualism (Pribble, 2013; Farías Antognini, 2019), generating segmented expansion. Argentina expanded effective access to health care in the 2000s by transferring funds to local providers to include uninsured patients (Plan Nacer/SUMAR), through the delivery of first-aid kits to health centers (Plan Remediar), and through the promotion of sexual and reproductive health. While these policies were a move toward more and better quality of health care, the fragmentation of the system along three pillars (public, private-insurance funds, and obras sociales [contributory insurance]) was maintained due to the strength and resistance of governors and provincial health ministers, as well as private actors and unions (Niedzwiecki, 2014).

While the importance of these legacies has a long tradition in political economy, scholars studying Latin America's expansionary phase have been innovative in their efforts to conceptualize and probe the effects of policy legacies in more systematic ways. One of the primary innovations of this research involves a careful conceptualization of the ways in which the entry of private actors during the neoliberal era has shifted the dynamics of social policy formation. Ewig and Kay (2011), for example, find that the strengthened position of private business interests during the neoliberal period helps explain the incremental character of expansion (Ewig and Kay, 2011: 68). For profit, private providers often developed strong corporate interests and became lobbyists. In countries where they were well organized, such as in Chilean health care, that was the case (Farías Antognini, 2019). To the contrary, in Uruguay, not-for-profit health-care private providers did not launch a campaign against the single payer model (Pribble, 2013). Similarly, in the case of childcare services in Chile and Mexico, the fact that private sector supply was weak and aimed at higher income families, facilitated the expansion of public childcare, which did not have to confront private interests (Staab and Gherard, 2011).

Where policy legacies strengthened corporate power and prerogatives, efforts to expand benefits often avoided confrontation with private actors, which in turn maintained existing segmentation. Pribble (2013) stresses that in Chile, private health insurance and private pension funds were created in a deregulated environment. In subsequent reform attempts, the private providers resisted efforts to regulate the provision of health services and oversight of pension fund administrators. This resistance meant that despite reforms, the underlying system maintained key characteristics that generated segmentation. In a similar vein, Huber and Stephens (2012) note that high levels of private spending on health and education in Latin America hardened elites against tax increases, making it difficult to improve the quality of public services. Martínez Franzoni and Sánchez-Ancochea (2016) show that the presence of an outside (market) option erodes public services. All of these examples point to the way that policy legacies that strengthened private actors made it difficult to reduce segmentation in education, health, and pensions, even during the expansionary phase.

Another innovation in the conceptualization of policy legacies is presented by Martínez Franzoni and Sánchez-Ancochea (2016), who use their concept of policy architectures to link policy design with legacies. They identify five dimensions of policy architectures: eligibility (the criteria to obtain a benefit), funding (who pays and how), providers (who provides and administers), benefits (who defines them and how), and the "outside option" (availability and regulation of market-based alternatives). Policy architectures create a set of opportunities and constraints for change. In another comparative paper, the authors analyze care policy and find that policy legacies are one of the factors that explain why Uruguay advanced further than Costa Rica in unifying policy architectures during recent years (Martínez Franzoni and Sánchez-Ancochea, 2019). In Uruguay, coverage was higher than in Costa Rica before the expansion in the 2010s (24 percent of the relevant population versus 5 percent) and included a mix of poor and nonpoor beneficiaries. Costa Rica's traditional providers were also regarded as excessively bureaucratic and inefficient, and reformers were skeptical about expanding them. In incorporating a myriad of local providers, the expansion of coverage generated increased fragmentation.

Policy legacies have also produced segmentation along gender and territorial lines. On the one hand, policy legacies have long-standing effects on gender segmentation, for instance, by making access to social protection (such as pensions) dependent on lifelong, full-time, and paid participation in the labor market. Thus, from the outset, these systems reflected gendered gaps in employment and earnings in terms of coverage and generosity (Martínez Franzoni and Mesa-Lago, 2003; Arza, 2012; Arza and Martínez Franzoni, 2018). Arza (2017), shows that some countries took actions to change features of policy design and enhance women's autonomous rights to a pension, but structural features that lead to gendered segmentation remained. Similarly, during the expansionary era, Argentina, Uruguay, and Brazil implemented policies to improve the social security coverage of domestic workers (90 percent of whom are women), but often by creating separate rules and/or programs, which resulted in different benefits for these workers compared to those in the private sector (Aguirre and Scuro Somma, 2010; Blofield, 2012; Rodríguez Enríquez and Marzonetto, 2015; Espino, 2016). This is a clear case of segmented incorporation, motivated by policy legacies: coverage of domestic workers expanded, but the history of policies that excluded such workers from the regular social security system meant that this expansion was done through separate systems with different (often narrower) rights and benefits for domestic workers. In a similar vein, CCTs contributed to segmented incorporation along gender lines. A legacy of social policies and gender norms that assume the male breadwinner/female caregiver model are embedded in this policy design. Therefore, while expanding women's access to cash benefits, CCT policies also reinforced gender-biased social norms.

Policy legacies also contributed to territorial segmentation in the expansion of social policies during the early 2000s. Niedzwiecki (2018) adds this new dimension to the concept of policy legacies by showing that subnational policy legacies influence the effectiveness of policy implementation. In the case of primary health policy in Brazil (*Estratégia Saúde da Família),* previous commitments to other health systems made the implementation of a new policy very challenging. In particular, in states and municipalities with a strong previous presence of hospitals and an alternative primary health system, the implementation of *Estratégia Saúde da Família* was more challenging than in contexts that never introduced the previous primary health system and that do not provide hospital-centered health care. All of this contributed to territorial segmentation with regard to the effective implementation of primary health policy.

The ways in which past policies matter also helps explain the unevenness of expansion across policy sectors. This is because the design of previous policies can incentivize action in some sectors, but discourage policy makers from engaging in other reforms. Pribble (2013), for example, notes that previous policies may generate coverage gaps that push politicians to expand a program to respond to unmet demands. The author argues that previous policies may also generate fiscal pressure, forcing politicians to take action. This, she contends, is one reason why Chile expanded access to health and pensions. It was also a motivation behind Uruguay's family allowance reform. Castiglioni (2018) notes that policy legacies can shape policy makers' perceptions of budgetary constraints and the fiscal cost of producing or failing to produce a reform, which can create unevenness across sectors in the type of reform adopted. Here, too, the evidence suggests that past policies can spur action in some domains, but also limit the scope of that action in others, thereby generating unevenness.

While policy gaps may generate new needs to be addressed, the reproduction of previous policy structures (who administers, finances, and provides benefits) and the logic for setting rights and benefits (who is entitled and to what kinds of transfers and services) help us understand why expansion happened in a segmented manner. Moreover, policy legacies shape preferences and ideas about how to deal with specific social problems, and expectations about the role of the state versus private actors, as well as attitudes about public spending. This is clearly the case regarding care services for young children and the boundaries between family and state responsibility, where long-standing notions that children should stay home get in the way of social demand for high-quality and extended ECEC services (Martínez Franzoni and Sánchez-Ancochea, 2018).

Taken as a whole, the literature on Latin America's expansionary phase agrees that the design of previous policies helps explain the nature of social policy expansion in the early twenty-first century. In our analysis of this literature, we find that policy legacies produced segmented expansion. Previous policies are popular, generate stakeholders and distribute power, produce gaps and new needs to be addressed, and reproduce gendered and territorial inequities. All of this contributed to segmented social policy expansion at the turn of the twenty-first century.

6 Explanatory Factors that Deserve Further Study

In our analysis of the literature on Latin America's expansionary phase, we identified two factors that have remained understudied: state capacity and international actors. Having a capable state is crucial for designing and effectively delivering policies, yet this factor has not been central to research on social policy expansion. The handful of studies that have begun to consider this variable explicitly, have generally focused on the subnational level. International factors, by contrast, received a great deal of attention in research on social policy reforms in the 1980s and 1990s, with scholars focusing on the role of international institutions like the IMF and World Bank and global networks of ideas (Work Bank, 1994; Huber, Mustillo, and Stephens, 2008). Yet these factors have received much less systematic attention in the literature of the 2000s.

Despite this lack of attention, in Sections 6.1 and 6.2 we show that there are reasons to believe that state capacity and international actors and ideas have influenced social policy in Latin America during the 2000s. Future research should consider these factors, contemplating how they might complement existing explanations or explain country diversity within the region.

6.1 State Capacity

State capacity refers to the ability of a state to control its territory and effectively implement policy (Skocpol, 1985). There is significant variation in the territorial reach of the state in Latin America, to the point that it is sometimes completely absent and unable to perform basic functions in important portions of the territory. This is what Guillermo O'Donnell (1993) referred to as "brown areas," that is, parts of a country's territory where the state is either absent, ineffective, and/or incapable of performing essential functions, where the rule of law is not guaranteed. In the total or partial absence of formal state structures, de facto local power systems fill the vacuum, providing basic public goods and allocating resources through particularistic and even corrupt practices (O'Donnell, 1993).

In this way, brown areas may open the way for social policies to be provided by nonstate actors. This is the case, for instance, in some Central American countries where informal institutions – from evangelical churches to youth gangs (*maras*) – play a role in providing public goods and services (Martínez Franzoni, 2008b; O'Neill, 2010). Churches might build schools and promote primary health in rural areas; gangs might look after mothers and widows of members who pass away. Rich (2019) shows that national government bureaucrats may attempt to overcome weak state capacity by supporting civil society organizations to advance public and social policies, something she calls state-sponsored activism. Although examples of nonstate collective allocation of resources can be found in all countries, they play a central and still understudied role in countries with exclusionary social policy regimes (Filgueira, 1998; Martínez Franzoni, 2008a; Cammett and MacLean, 2014). In these cases, as Holland (2017) has shown, authorities may also purposely fail to enforce the law to gain the electoral support of the urban poor, particularly when existing social programs are insufficient.

The literature on social policy reform recognizes that expansion requires that a state be capable of administering cash benefits and social services, but also of extracting revenue to finance the programs (Soifer, 2012). Countries with limited state capacity, therefore, may adopt a more restrictive range of policies than those with strong capacity, precisely because they are incapable of effectively performing the two functions. Weak state capacity may also be associated with insufficient infrastructure and restricted power to implement the policies that the government adopts. It is also linked to a gap between legally established social rights and the inability to guarantee their exercise (Duarte Recalde, 2014: 2). Overall, if the capacity of the state is limited, it is unlikely that governments will be in a position to adopt, implement, and/or sustain more ambitious social policies. This, in turn, could result in lower levels of coverage, access, and spending. Although, weak state capacity may inhibit the expansion of social policy and/or contribute to segmentation, the literature has generally failed to tackle this issue.[10]

Research focused on subnational variation in social policy pays more attention to the issue of state capacity. These studies suggest that weak state capacity helps explain implementation gaps and unevenness in expansion (Bonvecchi, 2008; Fenwick, 2009, 2016; Chapman Osterkatz, 2013; Pribble, 2015; Niedzwiecki, 2018; Wampler et al., 2020). Niedzwiecki (2018) shows that states with weak capacity are unable to successfully implement social policies and, in particular, basic health care. In contexts of weak state capacity, facilities are often in poor quality, lacking basic supplies, and/or do not meet basic requirements for people with special needs. These facilities are also understaffed because salaries are low and therefore trained personnel only stay temporarily and leave when they get a chance to find a better job. Finally, institutions in charge of providing health services are few and far between, especially in areas where they are needed most. As a result, people who live in remote areas often cannot access health care and/or the quality of the service provided is low, thereby generating territorial segmentation.

6.2 International Actors and Ideas

The role of international actors and ideas might also explain social policy expansion in the 2000s, yet, with a few notable exceptions, there has been little attention to these variables in recent work. As Bianculli et al. (2022) have emphasized, some key topics, such as social policy provision and regulation, have been virtually absent from the literature focusing on regional cooperation. While international actors and ideas were key for explaining neoliberal social policy reforms, they have received less attention in analyses of the expansionary era. This may be the result of the economic bonanza, which decreased the dependence of Latin American countries on external credit. In this section, we call attention to some of the ways in which international actors and ideas may have mattered, working via cooperation, diffusion, financial aid, and technical assistance.

One way in which international organizations may matter is through the development of discourses that encourage regional cooperation for social policy expansion. Mahon (2015) researched the role of the ECLAC in incorporating social policy into its neo-structuralist discourse in response to the shifts in the

---

[10] This omission is particularly noteworthy given that the past decade has generated crucial studies on state capacity in Latin American comparative politics (e.g. Soifer, 2012).

global discourse on social policy as well as the failure of neoliberal structural adjustment to deliver the promised benefits, as documented by ECLAC's Social Development Division. Artaraz (2011) highlights the role of ALBA (Bolivarian Alliance for the Americas) in encouraging networks of solidarity between Cuba and Bolivia for the expansion of health and education in the context of Bolivia's National Development Plan. Finally, Herrero and Tussie (2015) analyze the role of UNASUR's health council for the creation of health diplomacy in South America that aims at equitable health expansion through international cooperation. The authors refer to this phenomenon as the "unasurization" of health policies.[11] Additionally, the Millennium Development Goals of the United Nations in 2000, called for the adoption of a series of key measures to promote the eradication of poverty, including the universalization of basic education, the reduction of infant mortality, and the improvement of maternal health (UNDP, 2015). This may have led to coordination in the adoption of policies and instruments geared toward achieving these goals.

Policy diffusion is another way in which international actors may have influenced social policy expansion in the early 2000s, via the dissemination of models, policies, and ideas across countries and/or municipalities. The literature debates the relevance of external pressure, normative imitation, rational learning, and cognitive heuristics on the diffusion of different policies (Weyland, 2005; Osorio Gonnet, 2018a, 2018b). Neighboring countries learn from each other and face incentives to adopt good policies, especially when they are being promoted and advanced by international financial institutions (Borges Sugiyama, 2011; Brooks, 2015). In addition, left parties and socialized professional norms account for diffusion of good programs across municipalities in Brazil (Borges Sugiyama, 2013). In federal countries, diffusion can also go from the municipal or state level to decision-making at the national level (Béland, Medrano, and Rocco, 2018). All of this suggests that diffusion and learning are important areas to be explored in future research.

Besides cooperation and diffusion, international actors may also shape expansion by directly financing social policy through international loans. A good example of the relevance of international funding to facilitate the adoption of expansionary policies is Brazil in the mid-1990s, where a large World Bank loan helped increase the financial capacity of national AIDS programs significantly (Rich, 2019). International financial institutions, such as the World Bank and the Inter-American Development Bank, and more

---

[11] Despite the critical role of UNASUR, particularly to facilitate access to medicines in the early 2000s, by 2019, most member states had withdrawn from the organization, undermining its relevance (Bianculli et al., 2022).

recently, the government of China, have been important sources of loans for Latin American countries. Also, in terms of financial aid, south–south development assistance, promoted by a series of resolutions from the United Nations, increased the resources available for developing countries (Birn, Muntaner, and Afzal, 2017).

Evidence of the potential impact of international organizations and experts can be seen in the expansion of CCTs, childcare, and pension policies. In terms of CCTs, Osorio Gonnet (2018a) emphasizes the important role that experts, the epistemic regional community, and international organizations, such as the World Bank and the Inter-American Development Bank, had on the dissemination of these programs throughout Latin America. In fact, the first CCT programs were established in Mexico in 1997 and Brazil in 1998. Two decades later, as Morais de Sá e Silva (2017: 21) notes, forty-seven CCT programs were present in forty countries worldwide. International technical assistance facilitated this diffusion of CCTs. The endorsement of international organizations also helped spread CCT programs beyond Mexico and Brazil. Tomazini (2020) argues that the support for CCTs is, in part, the result of the formation of a pro-human capital coalition led by international financial institutions. These institutions were able to guarantee sufficient resources to maintain these programs, and played a role in convincing governments of the scientific legitimacy of the programs and promoting the projects domestically, to members of the pro-human capital coalition.

In terms of care policies, research finds that policy reforms were facilitated by the fact that care was featured on regional agendas and in networks with a gender focus (Esquivel and Kaufman, 2016). Martínez Franzoni and Sánchez-Ancochea (2018) argue that international consensus on the importance of quality childcare and early education for equality of opportunity, economic efficiency, and gender equality, helped frame the expansion of ECEC programs and services. Similarly, Sojo (2011) argues that these goals were present in the framing of ECEC programs launched in the 2000s in several countries. It remains to be established how interactions between national and international actors played out; that is, how policy innovations taking place in specific countries shaped the agenda of international organizations, which in turn created better conditions for domestic policies to expand. For instance, ECLAC closely followed and provided technical assistance related to the creation of the National Care System in Uruguay in 2013. Even though the creation of such a system cannot be attributed to ECLAC, once the Uruguayan system was launched, the international organization played a prominent role in disseminating the need for analogous systems elsewhere in the region.

In the realm of pensions, the World Bank's shift from advocating the privatization of contributory systems, as reflected in its 1994 *Averting the Old Age Crisis: Policies to Protect the Old and Promote Growth*, to endorsing the expansion of public systems, played a role in national agendas. More specifically, the agency went from promoting privatization to acknowledging the role of public funding and provision, and from strengthening contributory-based systems to also promoting noncontributory pensions. On the latter, the ILO's Social Protection Floor initiative has also been regarded as a relevant framework for promoting the expansion of social pensions across the region. The ILO 2011 Convention on Domestic Workers was also important for the expansion of social protection among domestic workers – as Blofield and Jokela (2018) show in their analysis of Brazil, Uruguay, Mexico, and Peru.

There is, therefore, evidence that international actors remained influential in the 2000s, though the scholarship pays less attention to these factors than during the previous wave of neoliberal reforms. More research in this area would be useful, especially regarding the interaction between international organizations and domestic networks. Future research could explore, for example, the mechanisms that link international institutions and actors with domestic partners (e.g. emulation, collaboration, conditionality), as well as the struggles between different international institutions to shape new social policies in Latin America and beyond.

7 Social Policy After the Expansionary Era – What's Next?

7.1 The Post-expansionary Phase

Following the expansionary period, Latin American social policy entered a new phase of stagnation. With declining commodity prices and slumping international demand, economic growth began to slow, reintroducing the need for fiscal adjustments (Nin-Pratt and Valdés Conroy, 2020). As shown in our analysis, the economic bonanza was not a sufficient condition for the expansion of social policy, but the availability of resources facilitated the process. Consequently, as public budgets have tightened, governments have been increasingly unable to maintain expenditure levels.

The ideological environment in several Latin American countries has also experienced important transformations since the end of the commodity boom. As the expansionary phase of social policy waned, several Latin American countries saw the rise of right-of-center administrations, including in countries where the left had a pivotal presence, such as Argentina, Brazil, Chile, Ecuador, and Uruguay. In Colombia, Honduras, Panama, and Paraguay, conservative presidents were reelected.

A number of Latin American countries also witnessed democratic backsliding/erosion after 2013. Brazilian democracy, for example, was weakened by the questionable impeachment of President Dilma Rouseff in 2016, while Nicaragua regressed to a hybrid regime. In Argentina, Chile, Costa Rica, the Dominican Republic, and El Salvador, IDEA reported that at least one sub-attribute of democracy declined during 2018 (IDEA, 2019). At the same time, public opinion polls show declining support for democracy across the region. According to the 2018 Latinobarómetro Report, only 48 percent of Latin Americans believed that democracy is preferable to any other form of government, whereas in 2010 that number was 61 percent (Latinobarómetro, 2018).

The combination of economic recession, ideological shifts, and democratic deterioration brought with it increasing malaise that placed social policies at the center of an intensification of distributive struggles. Indeed, waves of mass protest since 2013 have politicized social inequalities, highlighting problems of access to social programs, the insufficiency of income transfers, and the dismal quality of social services available to marginalized sectors. For example, in Brazil in 2013, protesters mobilized in response to increases in the cost of public transportation, but also demanded improvements to education and health services. In many ways, the protests confirmed the findings of scholars who criticized Brazil's social policy expansion, emphasizing financialization and the failure to guarantee social rights (Lavinas, 2014, 2017). Likewise in Chile, after more than a decade of mobilization aimed at improving social services and reducing inequalities, the country experienced an unprecedented social uprising (*estallido social*) in 2019. Protestors focused on many issues, but social vulnerability, inequality, and the limited scope of Chile's social protection system were among the most important factors that motivated participants. In Colombia, protests in 2019 focused on labor and pension reform, among other issues, and in 2021, Colombians took the streets again to protest against a tax reform widely perceived as regressive. While these protests help make social policy segmentation visible, they have not yet forced reforms that would move policy in a more equitable direction.

7.2 What the Pandemic Made Evident

On top of the difficulties created by the end of the expansionary era, the COVID-19 pandemic that began in 2020 has tested all Latin American nations. The pandemic has highlighted the importance of public goods and social services to people's lives and for resolving emergencies. It has also forced governments to adopt measures to prevent and confront the spread of the virus. In the domain of health care, states directed resources to vaccinating, testing, tracing, and treating COVID-19. Social distancing measures, such as lockdowns, travel restrictions, and school and business closures, among others, were adopted throughout the region. To make it possible for Latin American workers to stay at home and sustain themselves, different emergency measures were adopted, such as cash and in-kind transfers. Some countries relied on their existing CCT policies, others introduced new ad hoc mechanisms, and still others established transfers tied to their social security systems (Blofield, Giambruno, and Filgueira, 2020).

In terms of the topics addressed in this Element, the pandemic had at least two important consequences. On the one hand, it made the presence of the state and the adoption of new or expanded social policies more pressing than ever. In particular, governments deployed prompt responses, for instance in terms of emergency cash transfers aimed at an important proportion of the population. Although with differences in reach and generosity, this happened across the board, including in countries with a history of scarce social policy intervention, like those in Central America. Guatemala is a case in point (Martínez Franzoni, 2021).

On the other hand, the pandemic exposed serious problems related to the segmented character of social protection and labor markets in the region. More specifically, the pandemic and the adverse economic consequences that came with it, made the problems associated with the unequal access to social policies and formal employment evident. Latin America's high rates of informality meant that while a minority was able to keep their salaries and transition to working remotely, a majority worked in unsafe conditions, lost their jobs because tasks could not be performed online, and/or depended, at best, on emergency noncontributory transfers that were significantly lower and less predictable than labor income. Unequal and insufficient access to computers and internet connectivity also affected the ability to work and study from home, exacerbating existing inequalities. The pandemic also exposed inequalities in access to health care, emphasizing that even basic services, like sanitation, were still not available to all residents.

Relatedly, the ability to test, trace, and treat the virus, as well as the availability of intensive care unit beds and the delivery of vaccines, were hampered in countries with limited state capacity. More generally, the need to deal with such a complex scenario displayed the importance of having a strong state to perform these tasks. Uneven state capacity across and inside of countries, coupled with distinct configurations of public and private provision of care, generated access barriers in already unequal health systems.

Finally, the pandemic made visible the serious social consequences of neglected areas of state policy like childcare and the need to protect new social risks such as mental health. It also underscored the poor regulation of private actors, which limited the state's ability to monitor firms' compliance with employment regulations, including those specifically implemented to reduce the social costs of the pandemic (e.g. prohibition of layoffs and paid leave) and to enforce social distancing measures.

7.3 Did Pandemic-Related Policy Initiatives Challenge Segmentation?

On the bright side, governments throughout Latin America expanded existing cash transfers and implemented new ones in response to the pandemic (Blofield, Pribble, and Giambruno, 2022). In this vein, COVID-19 offered countries a unique opportunity to expand social policy while challenging segmentation, particularly in cash transfers and care policies. Emergency cash transfers reached a new population of beneficiaries that had previously fallen through the cracks, since those individuals were neither poor enough to qualify for social assistance, nor formally employed so that they could receive contributory social security benefits. In terms of care services, the pandemic created a blunt expansion of unpaid care demands, hand in hand with school closures, exhausted medical facilities and, overall, the contraction of all nonessential services. Altogether, the crisis not only created the opportunity to recognize care work but also created an expectation that the state will address this issue moving forward.

Though it is still too early to tell, it thus far appears that this opportunity may have been wasted. Insiders have been able to take advantage of policies tied to the contributory systems, while outsiders, who were harder hit by the pandemic and the economic crisis, suffered from collective action problems that constrained their capacity to mobilize grievances and demand new benefits. Thus, with a few exceptions, temporary emergency measures have not turned into permanent programs (Lavinas, 2021; Blofield, Pribble, and Giambruno, 2022).

Policy legacies are one of the reasons why government responses to COVID-19 have failed to reduce social policy segmentation. As we discussed in Section 5, policy legacies explain the segmented character of expansionary social policy in the early 2000s. Emergency policy responses to the COVID-19 pandemic also emerged in the context of existing programs and have thus far failed to break with historical segmentation. This was particularly problematic in the case of health care services. Before the pandemic, nearly a third of the Latin American population lacked access to health care for economic reasons, and around 20 percent because of geographic barriers (PAHO, 2015). Responses to COVID-19 built upon these existing inequalities that, heretofore, have remained unchallenged. The role of policy legacies can also partly explain why emergency cash transfers implemented in almost all countries during 2020, and which reach informal workers not normally covered, were short-lived in the midst of a crisis. Finally, if the favorable economic conditions that facilitated social policy expansion had already withered before the pandemic, fiscal space has further deteriorated during the COVID-19 crisis, constraining policy initiatives. When weighing the magnitude of the pandemic, the fact that governments were able to respond with expansionary measures – even if short-lived and even if unable to fight segmentation – is indeed remarkable. It is also quite possibly a legacy of the region's expansionary period.

Still, given the magnitude and multidimensional character of the pandemic shock, the role of legacies in what comes next remains to be seen. Might it be the case that the strength of legacies has been somewhat eroded, as the shock extends through time? Alternatively, might prepandemic legacies strengthen as countries move away from the shock? Given high public deficits, external debt constraints, and ongoing difficulties for raising taxes, there may be more reasons to be pessimistic than optimistic – at least for many Latin American countries.

8 Conclusion: What We Have Learned as a Compass for the Future

By 2013, Latin America had reasons for hope. After decades of structural adjustment, austerity and macroeconomic crises, the region had experienced a period of sustained economic growth and fiscal expansion. Many people saw improvements to their lives, as they were lifted out of poverty. Family incomes increased as a result of better labor market conditions and the expansion of public social benefits. New policies, including pensions and social assistance, as well as health and care services, reached groups who had previously been excluded, such as low-income families, self-employed and low-skilled workers, domestic workers, and informal workers, many of them women. Social protection coverage increased across the region under a new wave of social incorporation.

To account for these changes, a body of literature from different disciplinary fields analyzed social policy expansion in Latin America, developing novel concepts, multidimensional measures, and nuanced theories. The conceptual and empirical innovations brought by this literature improved scholars' analytic tools for characterizing and comparing social policy models across time and space. These advancements enhanced our ability to understand the politics of social policy, not just in Latin America, but also in other parts of the world, including advanced industrial democracies. In this Element, we built upon these contributions to characterize the ways in which expansion happened in Latin America. We also explored the factors that explain it. Our findings show that social policy expansion is multidimensional and that allowing for this complexity permits a fuller understanding of the real character of policy change. Specifically, we find that a focus on spending and coverage alone is insufficient, and that other policy features, including generosity, quality, and equity are key to understanding both the reach and the impacts of new social policies.

Social policy expansion in the early 2000s aimed to address some of the gaps and inequalities that have long characterized social protection systems in Latin America. Contributory social security systems, which developed during the second half of the twentieth century, excluded large groups of the population and mostly benefited formal urban workers. In the early 2000s, governments sought to change this reality, first and foremost by expanding noncontributory benefits like social pensions and CCT programs for poor families. Some governments also moved to incorporate new categories of workers under social security systems, cover new risks, ease access to contributory pensions, improve basic health care coverage, and expand childcare services. While means-testing remained widely used, particularly for cash benefits, some countries implemented less stringent eligibility criteria, and others pursued universal access. A novel feature of many new programs was that benefits were allocated in a nondiscretionary way. In addition, some states reduced the role of the market in service provision, as well as in previously privatized pension programs. In other countries, by contrast, the role of the private sector grew. Overall, notwithstanding variation in the breadth and depth of expansion across countries, there was a clear trend toward greater access to social policy across the board.

But did these reforms succeed at breaking with the unequal character of Latin American social policy? Not exactly. We argue that social policy expansion during the early 2000s was segmented across different population groups and policy sectors. It was also heterogeneous across countries. The extension of access and the improvement in generosity, where it occurred, generally maintained different "lanes" of incorporation for formal and informal workers and for the middle class and the poor. Thus, outcomes varied by labor market status and social class, by gender, race, ethnicity, immigration status, and region of residence (urban-rural). And while underprivileged populations have benefitted from expansion in most cases, historical patterns of social policy exclusion and inequality remain.

In terms of class and labor market status, the expansion of CCTs, noncontributory pensions, and basic health care did decrease access gaps, yet contributory health and pensions are still of better quality and more generous than noncontributory ones. In some cases, the difference between the two types of benefits is quite large. A similar trend appears when we focus on gender: women improved their autonomous access to resources, both due to labor market incorporation and greater access to cash benefits from new social programs. However, women continue to exhibit lower pension coverage and lower benefit values than men. Gender inequality issues have entered policy agendas and produced policy innovations in some countries, but several social programs continue to have a gender-biased, maternalistic designs, and childcare services remain underdeveloped. Segmentation by race and ethnicity also prevails, especially in terms of access, quality, and generosity. Immigrants face particular challenges for accessing good quality social policy, especially when policies require long years of legal residency or formal employment. This has translated into immigrants' lower access to pensions and health care when compared with citizens.

What explains this process of segmented social policy expansion? In this Element, we argue that democracy and favorable economic conditions facilitated social policy expansion, and that this expansion was segmented because of policy legacies. First, decades of democracy allowed social movements and left parties to organize and mobilize demands for social policy expansion. These demands, in turn, became more salient during elections and growing competition incentivized political elites to incorporate outsiders. Our finding reflects a broad consensus in the literature on Latin America's expansionary era that democracy can produce broader social protection, but that the process often takes time and requires the growth of civil society and left parties, as well as tightly fought elections. This lesson about *how* democracy influences social policy development is one of the many contributions that research on Latin America's expansionary era has made to the broader literature on comparative welfare states.

Second, favorable economic conditions in the early 2000s made it feasible to expand benefits. Economic growth and commodity boom, and a greater availability of international resources, gave governments the fiscal space to increase social spending. This made it possible to expand access and incorporate new beneficiaries without producing the distributive conflicts that had been characteristic of the region when austerity prevailed. In a context of greater fiscal space, the expansion of benefits for some groups did not entail cutbacks for others and all could benefit from welfare expansion in some way.

Third, the legacy of preexisting social policies promoted segmentation across social groups, sectors, and across the territory. Previous policies are generally popular among recipients, and therefore, prove hard to change, even when they create deep inequalities. This is the case because each group will resist losing its benefits. Past policies create stakeholders and may empower some groups over others. Past policies also create institutions that produce a certain distribution of rights and resources, build hierarchies based on class, gender, ethnic group, race, or region, and produce sector-specific dynamics that frame future policy reform. Finally, the design of previous policy shapes voter preferences and behavior, which in turn shapes political competition. Thus, policies that have been created in the past, with a particularistic design that provides different benefits to different groups, are hard to integrate into more universalistic models if the rights and benefits of powerful groups are at stake. Democracy and political competition generate a favorable context for new groups to demand benefits, but competition does not necessarily generate a push for an integrated, universal, and homogeneous system for all. Thus, democracy may simultaneously promote more access, better benefits, *and* segmentation.

Throughout history, Latin American social protection systems have gone through periods of expansion and retrenchment. In each of these waves, the legacies of previous policies have influenced subsequent changes, both limiting the scope of dismantlement during periods of retrenchment and limiting deep structural transformations during expansionary waves. Policy legacies – expressed in actors' ideas, interests, and power distribution, as well as in institutional structures, practices, and norms – frame policy reforms within boundaries that partly reflect and reproduce the status quo. But these legacies are themselves constructed and incrementally changed in the process of social policy reform. Accordingly, the expansion of social policy during the early 2000s created new stakeholders that now have a greater voice to defend their benefits – especially if democratic rule in the region survives. Similarly, the expansionary era lent social legitimacy to new ways of allocating state resources and benefits, shaping ideas that support demands for redistribution. These legacies, in turn, will likely shape future trajectories of policy change. Research on the diverse nature of policy legacies is one of the many contributions of Latin American literature for our understanding of the evolution of welfare states around the world.

If social policy was expanded in a segmented manner during the early 2000s, what happened after the expansionary wave? Since roughly 2013, most of the conditions that made expansion possible have either disappeared or been deeply challenged. With the end of the commodity boom, growth slowed and revenue contracted, while democracy also lost ground, with the region entering a period of backsliding. Moreover, the power of the left has weakened and a global pandemic is testing every social protection system in the world. While the context has changed, we believe that the accumulated knowledge about social policy expansion during the early 2000s can help us better understand this contemporary reality. Under the best light, the expansionary era generated new expectations and new demands on the state for more and better policies, which have not yet been fully met. This suggests that while the current era may push the region toward austerity, the process may not play out as it did in the 1990s because the experience of expansion created new politics that have transformed social protection systems – and expectations – in the region. For example, the politicization of inequalities and the *estallido social* in Chile could produce further expansion of social policy, perhaps even in a more universal direction, despite growing economic constraints.

At the same time, the politicization of inequalities through massive protests in Brazil, Chile, and Colombia also points to the limitations of the expansionary wave and its failure to break with historic inequalities. These protests, as we explained in the previous section, do not necessarily coalesce around demands for universalism and less segmentation, but reflect new, emerging demands and unmet expectations that the expansionary wave neglected. Overall, the growing social tensions and unmet demands that emerge in a less favorable socioeconomic and political context, raise new questions about the ways in which Latin American countries will manage the growing call for social incorporation in a context of increasing fiscal constraints and economic crisis.

The impact of the COVID-19 pandemic on social protection systems is still a pending question. The pandemic has produced devastating socioeconomic impacts across the region. Social indicators have deteriorated, with extreme poverty rising to levels not seen in more than twenty years (ECLAC, 2021a). Decreases in employment have disproportionally affected women, adding to their already weak position in the labor market and to their more limited access to work-based benefits (ECLAC, 2021b). The pandemic, and the context in which it emerged, have exacerbated structural inequalities that persisted in Latin America, even after the economic bonanza, making it clear that improvements to social protection systems remained imperfect. Across countries, government responses to the COVID-19 crisis have led to the creation of new social policies as well as the increased use of those developed and expanded during the early 2000s. These include cash transfer programs that were able to rapidly distribute benefits to impoverished populations. None of this, however, has been sufficient to address rising vulnerabilities and deep inequalities. Only a small share of the population maintained their salary levels and transitioned to remote work during the pandemic, while a majority have faced economic hardship and reliance on residual and unpredictable emergency transfers.

The global pandemic also highlighted issues that have not received sufficient attention in the literature about Latin America's expansionary wave, including the role of international power relations and actors, the weak regulation of the private sector, and problems of limited and uneven state capacity. In the realm of health care, debates on the role of the World Health Organization in the management of the pandemic, on the one hand, and agreements between rich countries and pharmaceutical companies, on the other, seem to suggest that international actors, corporations, and international power relations may matter for health policy in ways that are less visible during "normal times." A year into the pandemic, almost 90 percent of the COVID-19 vaccine was administered in rich and upper-middle-income countries, while only 0.1 percent was administered in low-income countries (Collins and Holder, 2021). The sluggish start of the vaccination campaign in Latin America was due, in no small part, to the concentration of vaccines in rich countries.

Finally, the experience of the pandemic calls for renewed attention to issues of state capacity; a factor that is somewhat neglected in the literature on the expansionary phase. The perils of weak state capacity became more evident in the management of the COVID-19 crisis, which required political and institutional coordination, planning, and evidence-based decision-making – all aspects of policy making that require a level of capacity that many Latin American states do not have.

Two decades after the beginning of the expansionary wave, news from the Latin American region points to several areas of concern for the future of social protection. Budgetary constraints, the erosion of democracy, increased social malaise, the rise of the right, and a global pandemic may prove detrimental to the region's ability to decrease segmentation or maintain the pace of expansion. There is also, however, room for hope. The expansion of social policies has "brought the state back in" to politics and distributive struggles. Structural socioeconomic inequalities have become increasingly politicized, thereby amplifying the voices of previously excluded actors and the emerging but vulnerable middle classes, who have taken to the streets to demand new or better benefits. The pandemic has also made it more evident than ever before that it is necessary to build stronger states, opening the way for the expansion of social policies, hopefully this time in a more equitable manner.

References

Agencia de Noticias Fides. (2007). Evo Morales afirma que la Renta Dignidad hará de Bolivia un país modelo. *Noticias Fides*. October 23. https://bit.ly/3PgyTxJ.

Aguirre, R. & Scuro Somma, L. (2010). *Panorama del sistema previsional y género en Uruguay: Avances y desafíos*. Serie Mujer y desarrollo 100. Santiago: CEPAL.

Alejo, J., Bergolo, M. & Carbajal, F. (2014). Las transferencias públicas y su efecto distributivo. La experiencia de los países del Cono Sur en el decenio de los 2000. *El Trimestre Económico*, 81(321), 163–198.

Altman, D. & Castiglioni, R. (2020). Determinants of Equitable Social Policy in Latin America (1990–2013). *Journal of Social Policy*, 49(4), 1–22.

Alves, J. (2015). (Un?) Healthy Politics: The Political Determinants of Subnational Health Systems in Brazil. *Latin American Politics and Society*, 57(4), 119–142.

Anria, S. & Niedzwiecki, S. (2016). Social Movements and Social Policy: The Bolivian Renta Dignidad. *Studies in Comparative International Development*, 51(3), 308–327.

Antía, F. (2018). Regímenes de política social en América Latina: una revisión crítica de la literatura. *Desafíos*, 30(2), 193–235.

Antía, F., Castillo, M., Fuentes, G., & Midaglia, C. (2013). La Renovación del Sistema de Protección Uruguayo: El Desafío de Superar la Dualización. *Revista Uruguaya de Ciencia Política*, 22(9), 153–174.

Antía, F., Castillo, M., & Midaglia, C. (2015). La estratificación como reto para los ajustes de los sistemas de bienestar. *Revista latinoamericana de investigación crítica*, 3, 101–135.

Arenas de Mesa, A. (2019). *Los sistemas de pensiones en la encrucijada: desafíos para la sostenibilidad en América Latina*. Santiago: CEPAL.

Artaraz, K. (2011). New Latin American Networks of Solidarity? *Global Social Policy*, 11(1), 88–105.

Arza, C. (2012). The Politics of Counter Reform in the Argentine Pension System: Actors, Political Discourse and Policy Performance. *International Journal of Social Welfare*, 21, 46–60.

Arza, C. (2017). Non-contributory Benefits, Pension Re-reforms and the Social Protection of Older Women in Latin America. *Social Policy and Society*, 16(3), 361–375.

Arza, C. (2018a). Cash Transfers for Families and Children in Argentina, Brazil and Chile: Segmented Expansion or Universal Benefits? *Journal of International and Comparative Social Policy*, 34(1), 58–75.

Arza, C. (2018b). Child-Centered Social Policies in Argentina: Expansion, Segmentation and Social Stratification. *Social Policy & Administration*, 52 (6), 1217–1232.

Arza, C. (2019). Basic Old Age Protection in Latin America: Non-contributory Pensions, Coverage Expansion Strategies and Aging Patterns Across Countries. *Population and Development Review*, 45, 23–45.

Arza, C. & Martínez Franzoni, J. (2018). A Long Decade of Gendering Social Policy in Latin America: Transformative Steps and Inequality Traps. In S. Shaver, ed., *Handbook on Gender and Social Policy*. Cheltenham: Edward Elgar, pp. 408–429.

Barba Solano, C. (2019). Welfare Regimes in Latin America: Thirty Years of Social Reforms and Conflicting Paradigms. In G. Cruz-Martínez, ed., *Welfare and Social Protection in Contemporary Latin America*. London: Routledge, pp. 29–58.

Barrientos, A. (2004). Latin America: Towards a Liberal-Informal Welfare Regime. In I. Gough & G. Wood, eds., *Insecurity and Welfare Regimes in Asia, Africa and Latin America*. Cambridge: Cambridge University Press, pp. 121–168.

Barrientos, A. (2009). Labour Markets and the (Hyphenated) Welfare Regime in Latin America. *Economy and Society*, 38(1), 87–108.

Barrientos, A. (2011). On the Distributional Implications of Social Protection Reforms in Latin America. *WIDER Working Paper 69*. Helsinki.

Barrientos, A. (2013). *Social Assistance in Developing Countries*. Cambridge: Cambridge University Press.

Barrientos, A. (2018). *Social Assistance in Low and Middle Income Countries Dataset (SALMIC)*. Global Development Institute, University of Manchester. Manchester

Barrientos, A. (2019). Social Protection in Latin America: One Region, Two Systems. In G. Cruz-Martínez, ed., *Welfare and Social Protection in Contemporary Latin America*. New York: Routledge, pp. 59–71.

Barrientos, A., Nino-Zarazua, M., & Maitrot, M. (2010). Social Assistance in Developing Countries Database Version 5.0. *Brooks World Poverty Institute Working Paper Series*, Chronic Poverty Research Centre Working Paper. Manchester. https://ssrn.com/abstract=1672090

Barrientos, A., Telias Simunovic, A., Fernandez, E. et al., eds. (2015). *Theoretical and Empirical Insights into Child and Family Poverty: Cross National Perspectives*. Sydney: Springer Nature, pp. 159–174.

Barros, R., de Carvalho, M., Franco, S., & Mendonça, R. (2010). Markets, the State, and the Dynamics of Inequality in Brazil. In L. López Calva & N. Lustig, eds. *Declining Inequality in Latin America. A Decade of Progress?* Washington, DC: Brookings Institution.

Béland, D., Medrano, A., & Rocco, P. (2018). Federalism and the Politics of Bottom-Up Social Policy Diffusion in the United States, Mexico, and Canada. *Political Science Quarterly*, 133(3), 527–560.

Bergman, M. (2019). Economic Growth and Tax Compliance in Latin America: Did the "Good Times" Help to Reduce Tax Evasion? In G. Flores-Macías, ed., *The Political Economy of Taxation in Latin America*. Cambridge: Cambridge University Press, pp. 53–75.

Berlinski, S. & Schady, N. (2015). *Los primeros años: el bienestar infantil y el papel de las políticas públicas*. New York: BID.

Bianculli, A., Ribeiro Hoffmann, A., & Nascimento, B. (2022). Institutional Overlap and Access to Medicines in MERCOSUR and UNASUR (2008–2018): Cooperation before the Collapse? *Global Public Health*, 17(3), 363–376.

Bird, R. & Zolt, E. (2015). Fiscal Contracting in Latin America. *World Development*, 67, 323–335.

Birn, A., Muntaner, C., & Afzal, Z. (2017). South-South Cooperation in Health: Bringing in Theory, Politics, History, and Social Justice. *Cadernos de Saúde Pública*, 33(2), 37–52.

Blofield, M. (2012). *Care Work and Class: Domestic Workers' Struggle for Equal Rights in Latin America*. University Park: Pennsylvania State University Press.

Blofield, M. (2016). Moving Away from Maternalism? Paper delivered at the RC19 Conference. University of Costa Rica, San José, August 26–27.

Blofield, M. (2019). The Politics of Social Policies in Latin America. *Latin American Research Review*, 54(4), 1056–1064.

Blofield, M., Ewig, C., & Piscopo, J. (2017). The Reactive Left: Gender Equality and the Latin American Pink Tide. *Social Politics*, 24, 345–369.

Blofield, M., Giambruno, C., & Filgueira, F. (2020). *Policy Expansion in Compressed Time: Assessing the Speed, Breadth and Sufficiency of Post-COVID-19 Social Protection Measures in 10 Latin American Countries*. Santiago: CEPAL.

Blofield, M. & Jokela, M. (2018). Paid Domestic Work and the Struggles of Care Workers in Latin America. *Current Sociology*, 6(4), 531–546.

Blofield, M. & Martínez Franzoni, J. (2014). Maternalism, Co-responsibility and Social Equity: A Typology of Work-Family Policies. *Social Politics*, 22(1), 38–59.

Blofield, M., Pribble, J., & Giambruno, C. (2022). The Politics of Social Protection during Times of Crisis. Unpublished manuscript under review.

Bonilla-Chacín, M. & Aguilera, N. (2013). *The Mexican Social Protection System in Health*. Washington, DC: World Bank.

Bonvecchi, A. (2008). Políticas sociales subnacionales en países federales: Argentina en perspectiva comparada. *Desarrollo Económico*, 48(190), 307–339.

Borges Sugiyama, N. (2011). The Diffusion of Conditional Cash Transfer Programs in the Americas. *Global Social Policy*, 11, 250–278.

Borges Sugiyama, N. (2013). *Diffusion of Good Government: Social Sector Reforms in Brazil*. South Bend: University of Notre Dame Press.

Brinks, D. M., Levitsky, S., & Murillo, M. V. (2019). *Understanding Institutional Weakness: Power and Design in Latin American Institutions*. Cambridge Elements. Cambridge: Cambridge University Press.

Brooks, S. (2015). Social Protection for the Poorest: The Adoption of Antipoverty Cash Transfer Programs in the Global South. *Politics & Society*, 43(4), 551–582.

Cabieses, B., Tunstall, H., Pickett, K., & Gideon, J. (2013). Changing Patterns of Migration in Latin America: How Can Research Develop Intelligence for Public Health? *Revista Panamericana de salud pública*, 34, 68–74.

Cabrera, M., Lustig, N., & Morán, H. (2015). Fiscal Policy, Inequality, and the Ethnic Divide in Guatemala. *World Development*, 76, 263–279.

CAF (2013). *RED 2012: Public Finance for Development: Strengthening the Connection between Income and Expenditure*. Caracas: CAF-Development Bank of Latin America.

Caldwell, K. L. (2017). *Health Equity in Brazil: Intersections of Gender, Race, and Policy*. Urbana: University of Illinois Press.

Calvo, E., & Murillo, M. (2014). Partisan Linkages and Social Policy Delivery in Argentina and Chile. In D. Abente & L. Diamond, eds., *Clientelism, Social Policy, and the Quality of Democracy*. Baltimore: The Johns Hopkins University Press, pp. 17–38.

Cameron, M., Hershberg, E., & Beasley-Murray, J. (2010). *Latin America's Left Turns. Politics, Policies and Trajectories of Change*. London: Lynn Rienner.

Cammett, M., & MacLean, L. (2014). Introduction. In M. Cammett & L. MacLean, eds., *The Politics of Non-state Social Welfare*. Cornell: Cornell University Press, pp.1–16.

Campello, D. (2015). *The Politics of Market Discipline in Latin America: Globalization and Democracy*. New York: Cambridge University Press.

Carnes, M., & Mares, I. (2009). Social Policy in Developing Countries. *Annual Review of Political Science*, 12(2009), 93–113.

Carnes, M., & Mares, I. (2014). Coalitional Realignment and the Adoption of Non-Contributory Social Insurance Programmes in Latin America. *Socio-Economic Review*, 12(4), 695–722.

Carnes, M., & Mares, I. (2016). Redefining Who's "In" and Who's "Out": Explaining Preferences for Redistribution in Bolivia. *The Journal of Development Studies*, 52(11), 1647–1664.

Castiglioni, R. (2018). Explaining Uneven Social Policy Expansion in Democratic Chile. *Latin American Politics and Society*, 60(3), 54–76.

Castiglioni, R. (2019). The Right and Work-Family Policies: Santiago. *Documento ICSO-UDP*, 58. https://icso.udp.cl/cms/wp-content/uploads/2019/08/ICSO_DT_58_Castiglioni_DEF.pdf

Castiglioni, R. (2020). La ampliación de políticas sociales bajo gobiernos de derecha y centro derecha en América Latina. *Revista Española de Sociología*, 29(3–2), 179–188.

Cecchini, S., & Atuesta, B. (2017). Conditional Cash Transfer Programmes in Latin America and the Caribbean: Coverage and Investment Trends. *Social Policy Series – CEPAL*, 224. https://cepal.org/en/publications/42109-conditional-cash-transfer-programmes-latin-america-and-caribbean-coverage-and

Cecchini, S., & Madariaga, A. (2011). *Programas de transferencias condicionadas: balance de la experiencia reciente en América Latina y el Caribe*. Santiago: CEPAL

Cecchini, S., & Martínez, R. (2012). *Inclusive Social Protection in Latin America: A Comprehensive, Rights-Based Approach*. Santiago: CEPAL.

Cecchini, S., Filgueira, F., Martínez, R., & Rossel, C. (2015), *Instrumentos de Protección Social: Caminoslatinoamericanos hacia la universalización*. Santiago: CEPAL.

Chapman, S. (2013). Commitment, Capacity, and Community: The Politics of Multilevel Health Reform in Spain and Brazil, PhD dissertation, Chapel Hill: University of North Carolina.

Ciccia, R., & Guzmán-Concha, C. (2018). The Dynamics of Redistributive Social Policy in Latin America, paper delivered at the *UNSRID Conference Overcoming Inequalities in a Fractured World*. Geneva: 8–9 November. https://bit.ly/3yWZNFt

Ciccia, R., & Guzmán-Concha, C. (2021). *Journal of Social Policy*, 1–22. doi:10.1017/S0047279421000623

Collins, K., & Holder, J. (2021). See How Rich Countries Got to the Front of the Vaccine Line. *The New York Times*. March 31, 2021. https://nyti.ms/3yzsO8O

Cook, M. L., & Bazler, J. C. (2013). Bringing Unions Back In: Labour and Left Governments in Latin America. *School of Industrial and Labor Relations Working Paper*. Ithaca: Cornell University.

Cookson, T. (2017). The Unseen Gender Impact of Conditionality: Extra-Official Conditions. *International Policy Centre for Inclusive Growth One Pager*, 345. https://ipcig.org/publication/28157?language_content_entity=en

Cookson, T. (2018). *Unjust Conditions: Women's Work and the Hidden Cost of Cash Transfer Programs*. Oakland: University of California Press.

Cornia, G., Gómez-Sabaini, J., & Martorano, B. (2014). Tax Policy and Income Distribution During the Last Decade. In G. Cornia, ed., *Falling Inequality in Latin America*. Oxford: Oxford University Press, pp. 295–317.

Correa Aste, N. (2011). Interculturalidad y políticas públicas: una agenda al 2016. *Economía y Sociedad*, 77, 53–58.

Cotlear, D., Gómez-Dantés, O., Knaul, F., Atun, R., Barreto, I. C. H. C., Cetrángolo, O., Cueto, M., Francke, P., Frenz, P., Guerrero, R., Lozano, R., Marten, R., & Sáenz, R. (2014). Overcoming social segregation in health care in Latin America. *The Lancet*, 385(9974), 1248–1259.

Cotlear, D., Gómez-Dantés, O., Knaul, F., Atun, R., Barreto, I. C. H. C., Cetrángolo, O., Cueto, M., Francke, P., Frenz, P., Guerrero, R., Lozano, R., Marten, R., & Sáenz, R. (2015). "La lucha contra la segregación social en la atención de salud en América Latina." *MEDICC Review*, 17, 40–52.

Cruz-Martínez, G. (2019). Esfuerzo de bienestar y pobreza desde el enfoque monetarista y de capacidades: Análisis transnacional en América Latina y el Caribe (1990–2010). *Política & Sociedad*, 52(3), 631–659.

Danani, S., & Hintze, S. (2014). *Protecciones Y Desprotecciones (II): Problemas Y Debates De La Seguridad Social En La Argentina*. Buenos Aires: Universidad Nacional de General Sarmiento.

De La O, A. (2015). *Crafting Policies to End Poverty in Latin America: The Quiet Transformation*. New York: Cambridge University Press.

del Pino, E., Sátyro, N., & Midaglia, M. (2021). The Latin American Social Protection Systems in Action. In N. Sátyro et al., eds., *Latin American Social Policy Developments in the Twenty-First Century*. Cham: Palgrave Macmillan, pp. 1–32.

de Sá, M., & Silva, M. (2017). *Poverty Reduction, Education, and the Global Diffusion of Conditional Cash Transfers*. Cham: Palgrave Macmillan.

Díaz-Cayeros, A., Estévez, F., & Magaloni, B. (2017). *The Political Logic of Poverty Relief: Electoral Strategies and Social Policy in Mexico*. New York: Cambridge University Press.

Dion, M. (2010). *Workers and Welfare: Comparative Institutional Change in Twentieth Century Mexico*. Pittsburgh: University of Pittsburgh Press.

Dorlach, T. (2020). The Causes of Welfare State Expansion in Democratic Middle-Income Countries: A Literature Review. *Social Policy &*

Administration, 1–17. https://onlinelibrary.wiley.com/doi/epdf/10.1111/spol.12658

Doyle, D. (2018). Taxation and Spending in Latin America. *Oxford Research Encyclopedia of Politics*. Oxford: Oxford University Press.

Duarte Recalde, R. (2014). Políticas Sociales y Democracia. *Nota de Debate*, 10.

ECLAC. (2019a). *Critical obstacles to inclusive social development in Latin America and the Caribbean*. Santiago: United Nations.

ECLAC. (2019b). *Non contributory social protection programs database*, ECLAC. Accessed April 30, https://dds.cepal.org/bpsnc/home.

ECLAC (2021a). La autonomía económica de las mujeres en la recuperación sostenible y con igualdad, Informe Especial COVID-19 N° 9, Santiago: United Nations.

ECLAC (2021b). *Social Panorama of Latin America 2020*. Santiago: United Nations.

Esping-Andersen, G. (1990). *The Three Worlds of Welfare Capitalism*. New Jersey: Princeton University Press.

Espino, A. (2016). Resultados de las reformas jurídicas relativas a las trabajadoras y los trabajadores domésticos en Uruguay. *Serie Condiciones de Trabajo y Empleo* No. 84. Ginebra: OIT.

Esquivel, V., & Kaufman, A. (2016). *Innovation in Care: New Concepts, New Actors, New Policies*. Berlin: UNRISD and Friederich Ebert Stiftung.

Etchemendy, S. (2001). Construir Coaliciones Reformistas: La Política de las Compensaciones en el Camino Argentino hacia la Liberalización Económica. *Desarrollo Económico*, 665–706.

Ewig, C. (2010). 3. Health Policy and the Historical Reproduction of Class, Race, and Gender Inequality in Peru. In L. Reygadas & P. Gootenberg, eds., *Indelible Inequalities in Latin America*. Durham: Duke University Press, pp. 53–80.

Ewig, C. (2012). The Strategic Use of Gender and Race in Peru's 2011 Presidential Campaign. *Politics & Gender*, 8(2), 267.

Ewig, C. (2015). Reform and Electoral Competition: Convergence toward Equity in Latin American Health Sectors. *Comparative Political Studies*, 49(2), 184–218.

Ewig, C. (2016). Gender Equity and the Politics of Health Sector Reform: Overcoming Policy Legacies and Forming Epistemic Communities. In J. Gideon, ed., *Handbook on Gender and Health*. Cheltenham: Edward Elgar, pp. 283–297.

Ewig, C. (2018). Forging Women's Substantive Representation: Intersectional Interests, Political Parity, and Pensions in Bolivia. *Politics & Gender*, 14(3), 433–459.

Ewig, C., & Hernández, A. (2009). Gender Equity and Health Sector Reform in Colombia: Mixed State-Market Model Yields Mixed Results. *Social Science & Medicine*, 68(6), 1145–1152.

Ewig, C., & Kay, S. (2011). Postretrenchment Politics: Policy Feedback in Chile's Health and Pension Reforms. *Latin American Politics and Society*, 53(4), 67–99.

Fairfield, T. (2015). *Private Wealth and Public Revenue in Latin America: Business Power and Tax Politics*. New York: Cambridge University Press.

Fairfield, T., & Garay, C. (2017). Redistribution under the Right in Latin America: Electoral Competition and Organized Actors in Policymaking. *Comparative Political Studies*, 50(14), 1871–1906.

Falleti, T. (2010). Infiltrating the State: The Evolution of Health Care Reforms in Brazil, 1964–1988. In J. Mahoney & K. Thelen, eds., *Explaining Institutional Change: Ambiguity, Agency, and Power*. Cambridge: Cambridge University Press, pp. 38–62.

Farías Antognini, A. (2019). *Políticas Sociales en Chile: Trayectoria de Inequidades y Desigualdades en la Distribución de Bienes y Servicios*. Santiago: UAH Ediciones.

Faur, E. (2014). *El Cuidado Infantil En El Siglo XXI: Mujeres Malabaristas En Una Sociedad Desigual*. Buenos Aires, Argentina: Siglo XXI Editores.

Fenwick, T. (2009). Avoiding Governors: The Success of Bolsa Família. *Latin American Research Review*, 44 (1), 102–131.

Fenwick, T. (2016). *Avoiding Governors: Federalism, Democracy, and Poverty Alleviation in Brazil and Argentina*. Notre Dame: University of Notre Dame Press.

Fides. Agencia de Noticias Fides. (2007). Evo Morales afirma que la Renta Dignidad hará de Bolivia un país modelo. Accessed May 1, 2021. www.noticias fides.com/nacional/politica/evo-morales-afirma-que-la-renta-dignidad-hara-de-bolivia-un-pais-modelo-14880.

Figueroa, M., G. M., & Tanaka. E. S. (2016). 'We Are Not Racists, We Are Mexicans': Privilege, Nationalism and Post-Race Ideology in Mexico. *Critical Sociology*. 42 (4–5), 515–533.

Filgueira, F. (1998). El nuevo modelo de prestaciones sociales en América Latina: eficiencia, residualismo y ciudadanía estratificada. Centroamérica en reestructuración. *Ciudadanía y política social*, 71–116.

Filgueira, F. (2007). Cohesión, riesgo y arquitectura de protección social en América Latina. In A. Sojo & A. Uthoff, eds., *Cohesión social en América Latina y el Caribe: una revisión perentoria de algunas de sus dimensiones*. Santiago: CEPAL, pp. 149–169.

Filgueira, F. (2013). Los regímenes de Bienestar en el ocaso de la modernización conservadora: posibilidades y límites de la ciudadanía social en América Latina. *Revista Uruguaya de Ciencia Política*, 22(2), 17–46.

Filgueira, F., Molina, C., Papadópoulos, G., & Tobar, F. (2006). Universalismo Básico. In C. Molina, ed., *Universalismo Básico: Una nueva política social para América Latina*. Washington, DC: BID y Editorial Planeta, pp. 19–58.

Flores-Macias, G. (2019). *The Political Economy of Taxation in Latin America*. Cambridge: Cambridge University Press.

Flechtner, S., & Sánchez-Ancochea, D. (2021). Why Is the Accumulation of Knowledge so Hard? Exploring Econometric Research on the Determinants of Public Social Spending in Latin America. *Latin American Research Review*.

Garay, C. (2016). *Social Policy Expansion in Latin America*. New York: Cambridge University Press.

Garcia-Subirats, I., Vargas, I., Mogollón-Pérez, A. et al. (2014). Barriers in Access to Healthcare in Countries with Different Health Systems: A Cross-Sectional Study in Municipalities of Central Colombia and North-Eastern Brazil. *Social Science & Medicine*, 106, 204–213.

Gasparini, L. G., Tornarolli, C. L., & Mejía. D. (2011). Recent Trends in Income Inequality in Latin America. *Economía*, 11(2), 147–201.

Gasparini, L. C., Cruces, G. A., & Tornarolli, L. H. (2016). Chronicle of a Deceleration Foretold: Income Inequality in Latin America in the 2010s. *Revista de Economía Mundial*, 43, 25–46.

Gibson, C. (2019). *Movement-Driven Development: The Politics of Health and Democracy in Brazil*. Stanford: Stanford University Press.

Gideon, J. (2012). Engendering the Health Agenda? Reflections on the Chilean Case, 2000–2010. *Social Politics*, 19(3), 333–360. https://doi.org/10.1093/sp/jxs009.

Gideon, J, & Molyneux, M. (2012). Limits to Progress and Change: Reflections on Latin American Social Policy. *Social Politics*. 19(3), 293–298.

Giuffrida, A. (2007). Racial and Ethnic Disparities in Health in Latin America and the Caribbean: A Survey. In A. Giuffirda, ed., *Racial and Ethnic Disparities in Health in Latin America and The Caribbean*. Washington, DC: IADB, pp. 1–22.

Giuffrida, A. (2010). Racial and Ethnic Disparities in Latin America and the Caribbean: A Literature Review. *Diversity in Health and Care*, 7(2), 115–128.

Gideon, J., & Molyneux, M. (2012). Limits to Progress and Change: Reflections on Latin American Social Policy. *Social Politics*, 19(3), 293–298.

Giraudy, A., & Pribble, J. (2018). Rethinking Measures of Democracy and Welfare State Universalism: Lessons from Subnational Research. *Regional & Federal Studies*, 29(2), 135–163.

Giraudy, A., Moncada, E., & Snyder, R. (2019). *Subnational Research in Comparative Politics*. Cambridge: Cambridge University Press.

Grugel, J., & Riggirozzi, P. (2018). Neoliberal Disruption and Neoliberalism's Afterlife in Latin America: What is Left of Post-Neoliberalism? *Critical Social Policy*, 38(3), 547–566.

Guendel, L. (2011). Política social e interculturalidad: Un aporte para el cambio. *Ajayu*, 9(1), 1–52.

Haggard, S., & Kaufman, R. (2008). *Development, Democracy, and Welfare States: Latin America, East Asia, and Eastern Europe*. Princeton: Princeton University Press.

Hemerijck, A. (2017). *The Uses of Social Investment*. Oxford: Oxford University Press

Hernández, T. (2013). Affirmative Action in the Americas. Americas Quarterly. Accessed May 27, 2021. www.americasquarterly.org/fulltextarticle/affirmative-action-in-the-americas/.

Herrero, M., & Tussie, D. (2015). UNASUR Health: A Quiet Revolution in Health Diplomacy in South America. *Global Social Policy*, 15(3), 261–277.

Holland, A. (2017). *Forbearance as Redistribution: The Politics of Informal Welfare in Latin America*. New York: Cambridge University Press.

Holland, A., & Schneider, B. (2017). Easy and Hard Redistribution: The Political Economy of Welfare States in Latin America. *Perspectives on Politics*, 15, 988–1006.

Hicks, T. (2009). *Strategic Partisanship Policy Seekers*. Ph.D. dissertation. Oxford: University of Oxford.

Huber, E., & Stephens, J. (2012). *Democracy and the Left: Social Policy and Inequality in Latin America*. Chicago: University of Chicago Press.

Huber, E., Mustillo, T., & Stephens, J. (2008). Politics and social spending in Latin America. *The Journal of Politics*, 70(2), 420–436.

Huber, E., & Niedzwiecki, S. (2015). Emerging Welfare States in Latin America and East Asia. In S. Leibfried, E. Huber, M. Lange, eds., *The Oxford Handbook of Transformations of the State*. Oxford: Oxford University Press, pp. 796–812.

Huber, E., & Niedzwiecki, S. (2018). Changing Systems of Social Protection in the Context of the Changing Political Economies since the 1980's. *Ciência & Saúde Coletiva*, 23(7), 2085–2094.

Huber, E., & Pribble, J. (2011). Social Policy and Redistribution under Left Governments in Chile and Uruguay. In K. Roberts & S. Levitsky, eds., *The Resurgence of the Latin American Left*. Baltimore: John Hopkins University Press, pp. 117–138.

Huber, E., & Stephens, J. (2015). Predistribution and Redistribution. Alternative or Complementary Policies? In C. Chwalisz & P. Diamond, eds., *The Predistribution Agenda. Tackling Inequality and Supporting Sustainable Growth*. London: I.B. Tauris, pp. 67–78.

Hunter, W., & Borges Sugiyama, N. (2009). Democracy and Social Policy in Brazil: Advancing Basic Needs, Preserving Privileged Interests. *Latin American Politics and Society*, 51(2), 29–58.

IDEA. (2019). The Global State of Democracy 2019: Addressing the Ills, Reviving the Promise. www.idea.int/sites/default/files/publications/chapters/the-global-state-of-democracy-2019-key-findings.pdf.

ILO. (2013). Domestic Workers across the World: Global and Regional Statistics and the Extent of Legal Protection. *International Labour Office*. Geneva: ILO.

ILO. (2021). ILO Social Protection Platform. Concepts and Definitions. Accessed January 12, www.social-protection.org/gimi/ShowWiki.action?wiki.wikiId=1113.

IMF. (1995). Social Dimensions of the IMF's Policy Dialogue. *World Summit for Social Development*. www.imf.org/external/pubs/ft/pam/pam47/pam47.pdf.

Korpi, W. (1989). Power, Politics, and State Autonomy in the Development of Social Citizenship: Social Rights during Sickness in Eighteen OECD Countries since 1930. *American Sociological Review*, 54(3), 309–328.

Korpi, W., & Palme, J. (1998) The Paradox of Redistribution and Strategies of Equality: Welfare State Institutions, Inequality, and Poverty in the Western Countries, *American Sociological Review*, 63(5), 661–687.

Lamprea, E. (2014). Colombia's Right-to-Health Litigation in a Context of Health Care Reform. In C. Flood, & A. Gross, eds., *The Right to Health at the Public/Private Divide: A Global Comparative Study*. Cambridge: Cambridge University Press, pp. 131–158.

Latinobarómetro. (2018). Informe 2018. *Banco de Datos en Línea*. https://latinobarometro.org/lat.jsp

Lavinas, L. (2014). 21st Century Welfare. *New Left Review*, 84(6), 5–40.

Lavinas, L. (2015). Anti-Poverty Schemes Instead of Social Protection. *Contemporary Readings in Law and Social Justice*, 7(1), 112–171.

Lavinas, L. (2017). *The Takeover of Social Policy by Financialization: The Brazilian Paradox*. New York: Routledge.

Lavinas, L. (2021). Latin America at the Crossroads Yet Again: What Income Policies in the Post-Pandemic Era? *Canadian Journal of Development Studies*, 42(1–2), 79–89.

Levitsky, S., & Roberts K. (2011). *The Resurgence of the Latin American Left.* Baltimore: The John Hopkins University Press.

Levy, S., & Schady, N. (2013). Latin America's Social Policy Challenge: Education, Social Insurance, Redistribution. *Journal of EconomicPerspectives,* 27(2), 193–218.

López-Calva, L., & Lustig, N. (2010). *Declining Inequality in Latin America: A Decade of Progress?* Washington, DC: Brookings Institution Press.

Lo Vuolo, R. (1995). *Contra la exclusión. La propuesta del ingreso ciudadano.* Buenos Aires: Miño y Dávila.

Lo Vuolo, R., ed. (2013). *Citizen's Income and Welfare Regimes in Latin America.* New York: Palgrave Macmillan.

Lo Vuolo, R. (2016). The Limits of Autonomy in Latin American Social Policies: Promoting Human Capital or Social Control? *European Journal of Social Theory,* 19(2),1–17.

Lustig, N. (2017a). Fiscal Redistribution and Ethnoracial Inequality in Bolivia, Brazil, and Guatemala. *Latin American Research Review,* 52(2), 208–220.

Lustig, N. (2017b). El impacto del sistema tributario y el gasto social en la distribución del ingreso y la pobreza en América Latina: Una aplicación del marco metodológico del Proyecto Compromiso con la Equidad (CEQ). *TrimestreEconómico,* 84, 493–568.

Lustig, N., Lopez-Calva, L.F., & Ortiz-Juarez, E. (2016). Deconstructing the Decline in Inequality in Latin America. In K. Basu & J. Stiglitz, eds., *Inequality and Growth: Patterns and Policy: Volume II: Regions and Regularities.* London: Palgrave MacMillan (and World Bank).

Lustig, N., & Pereira C. (2016). The Impact of the Tax System and Social Spending on Income Redistribution and Poverty Reduction in Latin America. *Hacienda Pública Española / Review of Public Economics,* 219 (4), 117–132.

Madrid, R., Hunter, W., & Weyland, K. (2010). The Policies and Performance of the Contestatory and Moderate Left. In K. Weyland, R. Madrid, & W. Hunter, eds., *Leftist Governments in Latin America: Successes and Shortcomings.* Cambridge: Cambridge University Press, pp. 140–180.

Mahon, J. (Forthcoming). Taxation, State Capacity and Redistribution in Latin America. In C. Arza, M. Blofield, & F. Filgueira, eds., The *Oxford International Handbook of Governance and Management for Social Policy.* Oxford: Oxford University Press.

Mahon, R. (2015). Integrating the Social into CEPAL's Neo-Structuralist Discourse. *Global Social Policy,* 5(1), 3–22

Malloy, J. (1979). *The Politics of Social Security in Brazil.* Pittsburgh: University of Pittsburgh Press.

Martinez, R., & Maldonado, R. (2019) Institutional Framework for Social Development. In R. Martinez, ed., *Institutional frameworks for social policy in Latin America and the Caribbean*. Santiago: ECLAC, pp. 21–47.

Martínez Franzoni, J. (2008a). Welfare Regimes in Latin America: Capturing Constellations of Markets, Families, and Policies. *Latin American Politics and Society*, 50(2), 67–100.

Martínez Franzoni, J. (2008b). *¿Arañando bienestar? Trabajo remunerado, protección social y familias en Centroamérica*. Buenos Aires: CLACSO.

Martínez Franzoni, J. (2021) Conferencia Inaugural Cátedra Humboldt, University of Costa Rica, April 26. https://bit.ly/3nUoJqN

Martínez-Franzoni, J., & Mesa-Lago, C. (2003). *Pensiones y Salud: Avances, Problemas Pendientes y Recomendaciones*, San José: Fundacion Friedrich Ebert.

Martínez Franzoni, J., & Sánchez-Ancochea, D. (2015). Public Social Services and Income Inequality. In J. Berg, ed., *Labour Markets, Institutions and Inequality*, Cheltenham: Edward Elgar, pp. 287–315.

Martínez Franzoni, J., & Sánchez-Ancochea, D. (2016). *The Quest for Universal Social Policy in the South Actors, Ideas and Architectures*. New York: Cambridge University Press.

Martínez Franzoni, J., & Sánchez-Ancochea, D. (2018). Undoing Segmentation? Latin American Health Care Policy During the Economic Boom. *Social Policy and Administration*, 52, 1181–1200.

Martínez Franzoni, J., & Sánchez-Ancochea, D. (2019). Overcoming segmentation in Social Policy? Comparing New Early Education and Child Care Efforts in Costa Rica and Uruguay. *Bulletin of Latin American Research*, 38 (4), 423–437.

Martínez Franzoni, J., & Voorend, K. (2012). Blacks, Whites, or Grays? Conditional Transfers and Gender Equality in Latin America. *Social Politics* 19(3), 383–407.

Martín-Mayoral, F., & Sastre, J. F. (2017). Determinants of Social Spending in Latin America During and After the Washington Consensus: A Dynamic Panel Error-Correction Model Analysis. *Latin American Economic Review*, 26(10), 1–32.

Mateo, M., & Rodriguez, L. (2015). *Who Cares about Childcare? Estimations of Childcare Use in Latin America and the Caribbean*. New York: BID.

Mayer-Foulkes, D., & Larrea, C. (2007). Racial and Ethnic Health Inequities: Bolivia, Brazil, Guatemala, Peru. In A. Giuffrida, ed., *Racial and Ethnic Disparities in Health in Latin America and the Caribbean*. Washington, DC: IADB, pp. 131–135.

McGuire, J. (2010). *Wealth, Health, and Democracy in East Asia and Latin America*. New York: Cambridge University Press.

Mesa-Lago, C. (1979). *Social Security in Latin America: Pressure Groups, Stratification and Inequality*. Pittsburgh: University of Pittsburgh Press.

Mesa-Lago, C. (2006). Structural Pension Reform—Privatization. In G. Clark, A. Munnell, K. Williams, & J. Orszag, eds., *The Oxford Handbook of Pensions and Retirement Income*, Oxford: Oxford University Press, pp. 663–683.

Montaño, S. (2011). Una mirada a la crisis de los márgenes. Cuadernos de la CEPAL 96, CEPAL, Santiago de Chile. https://cepal.org/es/publicaciones/27856-mirada-la-crisis-margenes

Molyneux, M. (2006). Mothers at the Service of the New Poverty Agenda: Progresa/ Oportunidades, Mexico's Conditional Transfer Programme. *Social Policy and Administration*, 40(4), 425–449.

Molyneux, M. (2009). Conditional Cash Transfers: A "Pathway to Women's Empowerment"? *Pathways to Women's Empowerment Working Paper 5*. IDS, University of Sussex. https://bit.ly/3AE0fKb

Molyneux, M., Jones, N., & Samuels, F. (2016). Can Cash Transfer Programmes have "Transformative" Effects? *Journal of Development Studies*, 52(8), 1087–1098.

Montenegro, F., & Acevedo, O. (2013). Colombia Case Study: The Subsidized Regime of Colombia's National Health Insurance System. Washington, DC: The World Bank.

Murillo, M., Oliveros, V., & Vaishnav, M. (2011). Economic Constraints and Presidential Agency. In S. Levitsky & K. Roberts, eds., *The Resurgence of the Latin American Left*. Baltimore: Johns Hopkins University Press, pp. 52–70.

Nagels, N. (2018). Incomplete Universalization? Peruvian Social Policy Reform, Universalism, and Gendered Outcomes. *Social Politics: International Studies in Gender, State & Society*, 25(3), 410–431.

Niedzwiecki, S. (2014). The Effect of Unions and Organized Civil Society on Social Policy: Pension and Health Reforms in Argentina and Brazil, 1988–2008. *Latin American Politics and Society*, 56, 22–48.

Niedzwiecki, S. (2015). Social Policy Commitment in South America: The Effect of Organized Labor on Social Spending from 1980 to 2010. *Journal of Politics in Latin America*,7(2), 3–42.

Niedzwiecki, S. (2016). Social Policies, Attribution of Responsibility, and Political Alignments: A Subnational Analysis of Argentina and Brazil. *Comparative Political Studies*, 49(4), 457–498.

Niedzwiecki, S. (2018). *Uneven Social Policies: The Politics of Subnational Variation in Latin America*. New York: Cambridge University Press.

Niedzwiecki, S. (2021). Welfare States and Immigration in Latin America: Immigrants's Inclusion to Social Policy in Argentina. *Kellogg's Work-in-Progress Seminar Manuscript.*

Niedzwiecki, S., & Anria, S. (2019). The Participatory Politics of Social Policies in Bolivia and Brazil. *Latin American Politics & Society*, 61(2), 115–137.

Nin-Pratt, A., & Valdés Conroy, H. (2020). After the Boom: Agriculture in Latin America and the Caribbean. *IDB Technical Note 02082.* https://publications.iadb.org/en/after-boom-agriculture-latin-america-and-caribbean

Noy, S., & Voorend, K. (2016). Social Rights and Migrant Realities. Migration Policy Reform and Migrants' Access to Health Care in Costa Rica, Argentina, and Chile. *Journal of International Migration and Integration*, 17(2), 605–629.

Ocampo, J. (2017). Commodity-Led Development in Latin America. *International Development Policy*, 9, 51–76.

Ocampo, J., & Gómez-Arteaga, N. (2016). Social protection systems in Latin America: An Assessment. *ILO Working Papers 994902513402676.* https://bit.ly/3PjNfNP

O'Donnell, G. (1993). On the State, Democratization and Some Conceptual Problems: A Latin American View with Glances at Some Postcommunist Countries. *World Development*, 21(8), 1355–1369.

O'Donnell, G. (1994). Ciudadanía, autoritarismo social y consolidación democrática. *Estudios Políticos*, 2, 167, 173.

O'Neill, K. L. (2010). *City of God: Christian Citizenship in Postwar Guatemala.* Berkeley: University of California Press.

OECD. (2020). *Enrolment Rates in Early Childhood Education and Care Services and Primary Education, 3- to 5-Year-Olds.* OECD Family Database. https://data.oecd.org/students/enrolment-rate-in-early-childhood-education.htm

Osorio Gonnet, C. (2018a). *¿Aprendiendo o Emulando?* Santiago: LOM.

Osorio Gonnet, C. (2018b). Comparative Analysis of the Adoption of Conditional Cash Transfers Programs in Latin America. *Journal of Comparative Policy Analysis: Research and Practice*, 21(4), 385–401.

Otero-Bahamon, S. (2016). *When the state minds the gap: the politics of subnational inequality in Latin America.* Ph.D. dissertation. Evanston: Northwestern University.

Otero-Bahamon, S. (2019). Subnational Inequality in Latin America: Empirical and Theoretical Implications of Moving beyond Interpersonal Inequality. *Studies in Comparative International Development*, 54(2), 185–209.

PAHO. (2015). *Experts Seek Ways to Boost Public Spending on Health in Latin America and the Caribbean to Achieve and Sustain Universal Health*. Pan American Health Organization. https://www3.paho.org/hq/index.php?option= com_content&view=article&id=11500:2015-experts-seek-ways-to-boost-pub lic-spending-on-health-to-achieve-sdg&Itemid=1926&lang=en

Perreira, K., & Telles, E. (2014). The Color of Health: Skin Color, Ethnoracial Classification, and Discrimination in the Health of Latin Americans. *Social Science & Medicine*, 116, 241–250.

Pierson, P. (1994). *Dismantling the Welfare State? Reagan, Thatcher, and the Politics of Retrenchment*. Cambridge, England, New York: Cambridge University Press.

Pierson, P. (2000). Increasing Returns, Path Dependence, and the Study of Politics. *The American Political Science Review*, 94(2), 251–267.

Pribble, J. (2006). The Politics of Women's Welfare in Chile and Uruguay. *Latin American Research Review*, 41, 84–111.

Pribble, J. (2013). *Welfare and Party Politics in Latin America*. Cambridge: Cambridge University Press.

Pribble, J. (2015). The Politics of Building Municipal Institutional Effectiveness in Chile. *Latin American Politics and Society*, 57(3), 100–121.

Pribble, J., & Huber, E. (2011). Social Policy and Redistribution: Chile and Uruguay. In S. Levitsky & K. Roberts, eds., *The Resurgence of the Latin American Left*. Washington, DC: Johns Hopkins University Press, pp. 117–138.

Reygadas, L., & Filgueira, F. (2010). Inequality and the Incorporation Crisis: The Left's Social Policy Toolkit. In C. Maxwell & E. Hershberg, eds., *Latin America's Left Turns: Politics, Policies and Trajectories of Change*. Boulder: Lynne Rienner, pp. 171–192.

Rich, J. (2019). *State-Sponsored Activism: Bureaucrats and Social Movements in Democratic Brazil*. Cambridge: Cambridge University Press.

Rinehart, C., & McGuire, J. (2017). Obstacles to Takeup. Ecuador's Conditional Cash Transfer Program, The Bono de Desarrollo Humano. *World Development*, 97, 165–177.

Rodriguez Enriquez, C., & Marzonetto, G. (2015). Organización social del cuidado y desigualdad: el déficit de políticas públicas de cuidado en Argentina. *Revista Perspectivas de Políticas Públicas*, 4(8), 103–134.

Rofman, R., Apella, I., & Vezza, E. (2015). Beyond Contributory Pensions: Fourteen Experiences with Coverage Expansion in Latin America. Washington, DC: World Bank.

Romero, W., & Orantes, A. (2017). *Estudio sobre racismo, discriminación y brechas de desigualdad en Guatemala*. México: CEPAL.

Rossi, F. (2015). The Second Wave of Incorporation in Latin America: A Conceptualization of the Quest for Inclusion Applied to Argentina. *Latin American Politics and Society*, 57(1), 1–28.

Rueda, D. (2005). Insider–outsider Politics in Industrialized Democracies: The Challenge to Social Democratic Parties. *American Political Science Review*, 99, 61–74.

Ruttenberg, T. (2019). Post-neoliberalism and Latin America. In J. Cupples, M. Palomino-Schalscha, & M. Prieto, eds., *The Routledge Handbook of Latin American Development*. New York: Routledge, pp. 111–120.

Sánchez-Ancochea, D. (2019). The Surprising Reduction of Inequality During a Commodity Boom: What Do We Learn from Latin America? *Journal of Economic Policy Reform*, (2), 1–24. https://tandfonline.com/doi/full/10.1080/17487870.2019.1628757

Sánchez-Ancochea, D. (2021). *The Costs of Inequality in Latin America: Lessons and Warnings for the Rest of the World*. London: I.B. Tauris.

Sala, G. (2017). Reorientación De La Política Previsional Argentina Y Acceso De Los Migrantes Limítrofes a La Seguridad Social. *Migraciones Internacionales*, 9(1), 119–149.

Segura-Ubiergo, A. (2007). *The Political Economy of the Welfare in Latin America. Globalization, Democracy and Development*. Cambridge: Cambridge University Press.

Sepúlveda, M. (2014). De La Retórica a La Práctica: El Enfoque De Derechos En La Protección Social En América Latina. *Serie Políticas Sociales – CEPAL*, 189, 1–74.

Silva, E. (2015). Social Movements, Protest, and Policy. *European Review of Latin American and Caribbean Studies*, 100, 27–39.

Skocpol, T. (1985). Bringing the State Back In: Strategies of Analysis in Current Research. In P. Evans, D. Rueschemeyer, & S. Skocpol, eds., *Bringing the State Back*. Cambridge: Cambridge University Press, pp. 3–43.

Smith, P. (2012). *Democracy in Latin America: Political Change in Comparative Perspective*. Oxford: Oxford University Press.

Soifer, H. (2012). Measuring State Capacity in Contemporary Latin America. *Revista de Ciencia Política*, 32(3), 585–598.

Sojo, A. (2011). De la evanescencia a la mira: el cuidado como eje de políticas y de actores en América Latina. *Serie Seminarios y Conferencias – CEPAL*, 67, 1–70.

Sojo, A. (2017). *Protección social en América Latina: la desigualdad en el banquillo*. Santiago: United Nations.

Staab, S. (2012). Maternalism, Male-Breadwinner Bias, and Market Reform: Historical Legacies and Current Reforms in Chilean Social Policy. *Social Politics*, 19(3), 299–332.

Staab, S. (2016). Opportunities and Constraints on Gender-Egalitarian Policy Change: Michelle Bachelet's Social Protection Agenda (2006–2010). In G. Waylen, ed., *Gender, Institutions, and Change in Bachelet's Chile*. London: Institute of the Americas, pp. 121–146.

Staab, S., & Gherard, R. (2010). *Childcare Expansion in Chile and Mexico: For Women or Children or Both?* Geneva: UNRISD.

Staab, S., & Gerhard, R. (2011). Putting Two and Two Together? Early Childhood Education, Mothers' Employment and Care Service Expansion in Chile and Mexico. *Development and Change*, 42(4), 1079–1107.

Telles, E., & Paixão, M. (2013). Affirmative Action in Brazil. *LASA Forum*, XLIV(2), 10–11.

Tillin, L., & Duckett, J. (2017). The Politics of Social Policy: Welfare Expansion in Brazil, China, India and South Africa in Comparative Perspective. *Commonwealth & Comparative Politics*, 55(3), 253–277.

Tomazini, C. (2020). Esquiver les critiques: les institutions financières internationals face aux politiques de lutte contre la pauvreté au Brésil et au Mexique. *Critique Internationale*, 3(88), 51–70.

Wampler, B., Sugiyama, N., & Touchton, M. (2020). *Democracy at Work: Pathways to Well-Being in Brazil*. Cambridge: Cambridge University Press.

UNDP. (2015). Objetivos de Desarrollo del Milenio. Informe de 2015. https://undp .org/sites/g/files/zskgke326/files/publications/es/UNDP_MDG_Report_2015 .pdf

UNDP. (2019). *Human Development Report 2019. Beyond Income, Beyond Averages, Beyond Today: Inequalities in Human Development in the 21st Century*. New York: United Nations Development Programme.

Uribe-Gómez, M. (2017). Nuevos cambios, viejos esquemas: las políticas de salud en México y Colombia en los años 2000. *Cadernos de Saúde Pública*, 33(2), 1–12.

Vieira, R. S., & Arends-Kuenning, M. (2019). Affirmative Action in Brazilian Universities: Effects on the Enrollment of Targeted Groups. *Economics of Education Review*, 73, 10–11.

Voorend, K. (2019). *¿Un imán de bienestar en el Sur? Migración y política social en Costa Rica*. San José: Universidad de Costa Rica.

Wampler, B., Borges Sugiyama, N., & Touchton, M. (2019). *Democracy at Work: Pathways to Well-Being in Brazil*. Cambridge: Cambridge University Press.

Weible, K., Böger, T., & Berten, J. (2015). *FLOORCASH-Basic. The Basic Dataset on Social Cash Transfers in the Global South, Version 2*. Research Project FLOOR (FloorCash). Germany: Bielefeld University.

Weitz-Shapiro, R. (2014). *Curbing Clientelism in Argentina: Politics, Poverty, and Social Policy*. Cambridge: Cambridge University Press.

Weyland, K. (2005). Theories of Policy Diffusion: Lessons from Latin American Pension Reform. *World Politics*, 57, 262–295.

Weyland, K., de la Madrid, R., & Hunter, W. (2010). *Leftist Governments in Latin America*. Cambridge: Cambridge University Press.

Williamson, J. (2000). What Should the World Bank Think About the Washington Consensus? *The World Bank Research Observer*, 15(2), 251–264.

World Bank. (1994). *Averting the Old Age Crisis: Policies to Protect the Old and Promote Growth*. Oxford: Oxford University Press.

World Bank. (2019). *ASPIRE: The Atlas of Social Protection Indicators of Resilience and Equity*. The World Bank. Accessed on February 16, 2020. https://www.worldbank.org/en/data/datatopics/aspire.

Zarate Tenorio, B. (2014). Social Spending Responses to Organized Labor and Mass Protests in Latin America, 1970–2007. *Comparative Political Studies*, 47(14), 1945–1972.

Acknowledgments

This project emerged out of collaboration via the Red Latinoamericana de Análisis de la Política Social, www.PolSoc.org. We would like to thank Evelyne Huber, Kent Eaton, Fernando Filgueira, Nate Edenhofer, Candelaria Garay, Mark Massoud, Eleonora Pasotti, Ben Read, Roger Schoenman, Thomas Serres, Tiago Tasca, Lucia Vitale, our colleagues from PolSoc, the editors of the Elements Series, and the two anonymous reviewers for their excellent comments on previous versions of the text. Camilo García and Diego Rojas provided crucial research assistance. This Element received funding from Fondo concursante de Redes Temáticas, Universidad de Costa Rica, Proyecto ¿Continuidad o refundación? La política social latinoamericana luego de la década expansiva (2000–2013), B9719 and from FONDECYT project 1180184. We also thank the support of our home institutions.

Politics and Society in Latin America

Maria Victoria Murillo

Columbia University

Maria Victoria Murillo is Professor of Political Science and International Affairs at Columbia University. She is the author of *Political Competition, Partisanship, and Policymaking in the Reform of Latin American Public Utilities* (Cambridge, 2009). She is also editor of *Carreras Magisteriales, Desempeño Educativo y Sindicatos de Maestros en América Latina* (2003), and co-editor of *Argentine Democracy: The Politics of Institutional Weakness* (2005). She has published in edited volumes as well as in the *American Journal of Political Science, World Politics*, and *Comparative Political Studies*, among others.

Tulia G. Falleti

University of Pennsylvania

Tulia G. Falleti is the Class of 1965 Endowed Term Professor of Political Science, Director of the Center for Latin American and Latinx Studies, and Senior Fellow of the Leonard Davis Institute for Health Economics at the University of Pennsylvania. She received her BA in Sociology from the Universidad de Buenos Aires and her Ph.D. in Political Science from Northwestern University. Falleti is the author of *Decentralization and Subnational Politics in Latin America* (Cambridge University Press, 2010), which earned the Donna Lee Van Cott Award for best book on political institutions from the Latin American Studies Association, and with Santiago Cunial of *Participation in Social Policy: Public Health in Comparative Perspective* (Cambridge University Press, 2018). She is co-editor, with Orfeo Fioretos and Adam Sheingate, of *The Oxford Handbook of Historical Institutionalism* (Oxford University Press, 2016), among other edited books. Her articles on decentralization, federalism, authoritarianism, qualitative methods, and Indigenous Peoples' politics have appeared in edited volumes and journals such as the *American Political Science Review, Comparative Political Studies, Publius, Studies in Comparative International Development*, and *Qualitative Sociology*, among others.

Juan Pablo Luna

The Pontifical Catholic University of Chile

Juan Pablo Luna is Professor of Political Science at The Pontifical Catholic University of Chile. He received his BA in Applied Social Sciences from the UCUDAL (Uruguay) and his PhD in Political Science from the University of North Carolina at Chapel Hill. He is the author of *Segmented Representation. Political Party Strategies in Unequal Democracies* (Oxford University Press, 2014), and has co-authored *Latin American Party Systems* (Cambridge University Press, 2010). In 2014, along with Cristobal Rovira, he co-edited *The Resilience of the Latin American Right* (Johns Hopkins University). His work on political representation, state capacity, and organized crime has appeared in the following journals: *Comparative Political Studies, Revista de Ciencia Política*, the *Journal of Latin American Studies, Latin American Politics and Society, Studies in Comparative International Development, Política y Gobierno, Democratization, Perfiles Latinoamericanos*, and the *Journal of Democracy*.

Andrew Schrank

Brown University

Andrew Schrank is the Olive C. Watson Professor of Sociology and International & Public Affairs at Brown University. His articles on business, labor, and the state in Latin America have appeared in the *American Journal of Sociology, Comparative Politics, Comparative*

Political Studies, Latin American Politics & Society, Social Forces, and *World Development,* among other journals, and his co-authored book, *Root-Cause Regulation: Labor Inspection in Europe and the Americas,* is forthcoming at Harvard University Press.

Advisory Board

About the Series

Latin American politics and society are at a crossroads, simultaneously confronting serious challenges and remarkable opportunities that are likely to be shaped by formal institutions and informal practices alike. The Elements series on Politics and Society in Latin America offers multidisciplinary and methodologically pluralist contributions on the most important topics and problems confronted by the region.

Cambridge Elements ≡

Politics and Society in Latin America

A full series listing is available at: www.cambridge.org/PSLT